Not-So-Simple Picture Books:
Developing responses to literature with 4–12 year olds

Not-So-Simple Picture Books: Developing responses to literature with 4–12 year olds

Pam Baddeley and Chris Eddershaw

tb

Trentham Books

First published in 1994 by Trentham Books Limited

Reprinted 1996

Trentham Books Limited
Westview House
734 London Road
Oakhill
Stoke-on-Trent
Staffordshire
England ST4 5NP

British Library Cataloguing Publication Data
A catalogue record for this book is available from the British Library.

ISBN: 0 948080 79 5 ✓

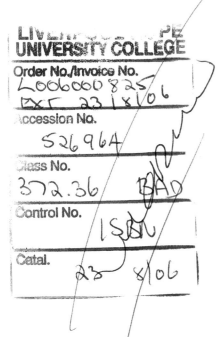
Designed and typeset by Trentham Print Design Limited and printed by Bemrose Shafron Limited, Chester.

We would like to thank all those who have helped and advised us, especially Clare Benningwood, Frieda Haynes and Peter Twining. We would also like to thank the children in the Gloucestershire primary schools with whom we worked.

Contents

Introduction

> *Each re-reading ... of a text is an act of reinterpretation and therefore interesting as development in thinking.*
> (Margaret Meek 1992 p.15)

Picture books can be deceptive. There may be more to them than first meets the eye. Good picture books deal with important human issues and can convey quite complex ideas despite their economic use of words. An apparently simple, humorous book like *Not Now Bernard*, for instance, allows children to explore parental love:

> Harry: *It doesn't mean they care if they make food for them or give them toys, caring's about loving them and stuff not just giving them toys and giving them food....*

Not only can books promote this quality of response, they can also encourage children to begin reading the subtext. The best picture books are open to interpretation because they leave so much unsaid. Coming to terms with the subtext demands from children a high level of thinking, but with sensitive teacher intervention they can gain considerable insight into what lies beneath the apparently simple surface of a book. In *The Not-so-Wicked Stepmother* there is a telephone conversation in which the little girl Hessie and her Mother do not say what they are really feeling. Yet children are able to identify with the unspoken text:

> Teacher: *So you've noted ('I wouldn't be so happy that Hessie's having a good time') what Mum might be possibly feeling, but she's not saying it is she?*

> Lisa: *She might hurt Hessie and she wants Hessie to have a good time while she can.*

Because the National Curriculum only mentions picture books in Key Stage 1, it has perhaps unwittingly given support to the general feeling that picture books are lightweight and only for younger readers. There are now sufficient good picture books on the market (see Appendix 2) for teachers to provide eleven year olds as well as four year olds with very rich reading experiences.

Although the text of these books is simple, the meaning behind them is not, and the older the child the greater their insight will be into the meaning. We intend to demonstrate that good picture books by their very nature cater for the detailed provisions of the programmes of study for Key Stage 2 also. We discuss a number of books we have used in school, showing how their quality excites and challenges children to reflect on their own and other people's experience, and on the ways in which language is used. We hope it is obvious that the response of the older children was excitingly mature and that the books were preparing them for coping with the complexities of more demanding texts at later stages of their development as readers. This account illustrates that good picture books can do far more than merely satisfy the demands of the primary English Curriculum.

In Chapter one we show how even the simplest form of picture book (with no text) can be less simple than it appears. They are often regarded as straightforward enough for children to look at on their own, because they have no print and anyone can follow pictures! But in textless picture books the task of telling the story is passed to the reader. Unless children can understand the conventions in all their variations that illustrators employ, they will have difficulty understanding the story. Consequently, they might miss a good deal of what the story is about and even reject it. Sometimes illustrators depict two events simultaneously so children need to be alert to this and able to see the relationship between the two narratives.

When text is added to picture books, children have to read text and pictures together and be aware of the interplay between them. Chapter two discusses some of the better picture books in which the pictures do not simply mirror the text but often add to, extend or even contradict it.

The economy of words characteristic of these books — misleading people into thinking they are simple — is achieved by indicating through picture things left unsaid or difficult to convey through words. Or the combination of text and picture might be sufficiently potent to suggest much else left unspoken. So children need to be alert to the tension between what the text says and what the pictures actually show, and have also to be able to read the subtext.

These are not simple skills for inexperienced readers.

Picture books can certainly be appreciated and enjoyed at a superficial level; however, even infants are capable of more than that, if teachers can be encouraged to find ways of helping them to respond thoughtfully to what books have to offer. Chapter three illustrates the kinds of questions that teachers might ask infants in order to develop more thoughtful responses. It also indicates how the questions might be extended for older children when they revisit a good picture book. It suggests some strategies for teachers to overcome older children's possible initial opposition towards picture books, and concludes with an example of how picture books can be thematically linked.

The advantages for older children of revisiting familiar stories is demonstrated in Chapter four. Ten and eleven year olds enthusiastically discuss modern picture book versions of traditional fairy stories. We see how the power of the illustrations enables the children to appreciate a familiar story in a new way and to find deeper layers of meaning. There is real excitement amongst these children when they became aware of the symbolism of the bars and the rainbow in Anthony Browne's *Hansel and Gretel*, for instance.

Chapter four also illustrates how children of this age can be encouraged by modern picture book versions of traditional tales to develop their ability to empathise and parody. Starting with someone else's raw material and shaping it to give a new dimension to the meaning, helped children towards an awareness of the power of language. They realised that by slanting stories in certain ways it was possible to give a whole new meaning to the text. The chapter concludes with an example of a series of picture books, linked by the theme of 'the stepmother', deepening children's awareness of relationships and helping them to look beneath the stereotype to find the individual.

Chapter five focuses on one picture book and how it stimulates lively discussion amongst a group of children left on their own. It highlights the importance of the role of the teacher in initiating the discussion and extending the children's ideas when he joins the group later in the lesson. The children's talk is assessed and their capacity for self-assessment demonstrated.

Chapter six concentrates on the fun children have exploring the humorous use of language in picture books, showing the significant contribution that books can make to children's growing sensitivity towards language, while simultaneously enhancing their enjoyment. It argues that this will only happen if older children are encouraged to return to picture books at a time when their own sense of humour is sufficiently developed. With sensitive teacher intervention, the author's use of imagery, irony and parody are brought within the grasp of older children. This understanding will lead to a deeper appreciation than children could achieve when they were five.

The final chapter draws attention to a book which epitomises all we believe that picture books can do for developing children's thinking right across the age range. *John Brown, Rose and The Midnight Cat* is a simple enough story but it can engage the reader's emotions at the deepest level. Children and adults have difficulty remaining neutral about the characters once the teacher has opened up the possible ways of interpreting this story, with its enigmatic ending.

We hope that the excitement and involvement of the children working with good picture books comes across to the reader, and that it will encourage other teachers to work in similar ways.

Reference

Meek, M. (1992) *Transitions: the notion of change in writing for children*. Signal No 67, Thimble Press.

CHAPTER 1

'How do you read that bit?'
Reading the conventions

Many picture books have the air of refusing to take anything for granted; they seem to assume an audience for whom the shape and nature of much in the world, especially the activity called reading, is still in flux. (Lewis, 1990 p.142)

Fully understanding the story in the best picture books depends mainly upon the reader's ability to interpret the pictures. This applies still more to textless picture books, often considered the simplest form of story. Yet these might in fact pose particular problems for young children who are unfamiliar with the conventions used by illustrators. The very absence of text can be problematic for children unaccustomed to such books.

Nicola (3 years):	*Mm, I mean, how do you read that bit?*
Teacher:	*How do you read this book? Why did you ask that?*
Nicola:	*Cos it hasn't got any numbers, that picture.*

Picture books without words might be rejected as too simple or as less important than books with words. This is a view we would like to challenge. In many textless books, the apparent simplicity masks a sophistication which may demand of young children skills underestimated by adults. The devices these storytellers use are inventive and subtle; they require concentration, interpretation, a knowledge of symbols, an eye for detail and an understanding of certain conventions. To appreciate fully the way these pictures 'tell' the story, young children will need the sensitive support of an adult who can help them to extract meaning from the pictures; they will also need opportunities to revisit the books and re-interpret them in the light of new experience.

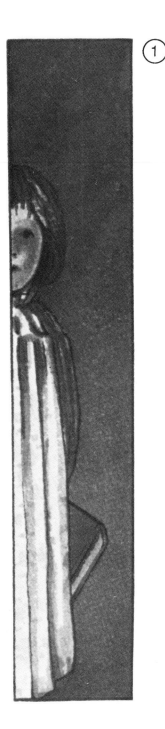

①

Apparently simple pictures may cause confusion for very young children, such as the picture on the second page of *Sunshine*, showing just one half of a little girl (illustration 1). Experienced readers will realise she is peeping round the door at her sleeping parents, but a young child might wonder where the other half of her is. The potential for confusion is considerable in even simple representations. One three year old, looking at a picture in the same book of Dad in bed glancing at his watch, thought the position of his hand indicated that he was 'holding Mum'.

Understanding conventions of perspective is not something that children under five will normally have grasped, so textless picture books like *The Angel and the Soldier Boy* and *Little Pickle* can be confusing.

In the latter a sequence of pictures shows a dinghy with a little girl in it, growing smaller and smaller as it drifts out to sea (illustration 2). Some children see this as five different size boats and not one moving away. Even when four year old Katie does appear to have grasped the concept, she still faces

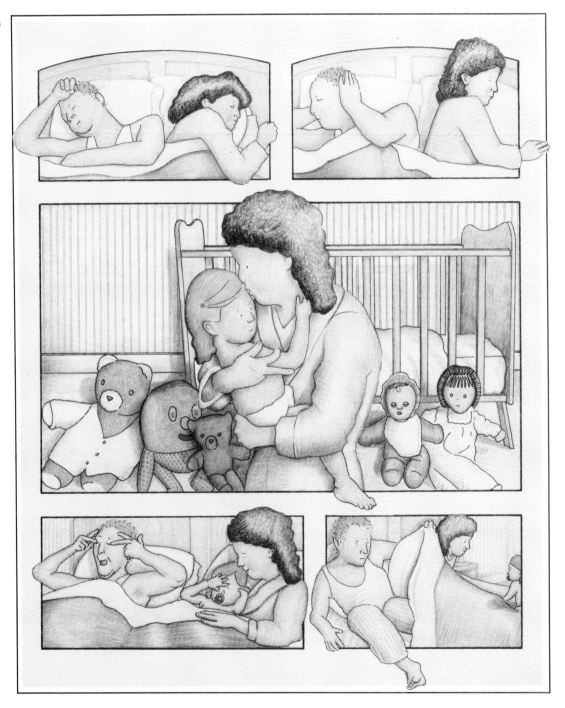

the challenge of expressing her understanding in words: witness her re-telling the story of the pictures to a four year old friend who did not understand!

> Katie: *And she got into the boat and it was nearer and near away and further and away.*

One common device found in textless picture books is a series of boxed pictures going from left to right and top to bottom, on the same page. This requires a completely different way of looking at pictures from the global eye movements normally used to scan a picture. Children need to know that the pictures follow a certain order and that the meaning is extracted by following this order. Even when a child knows where to start reading the pictures, the natural tendency for the eye to go to the right-hand page before the left may override this knowledge. When asked where you start, Katie pointed correctly to the top left hand picture. Re-telling the story of *Little Pickle* however, she turned from one right-hand page to the next, missing out the intervening left-hand page.

The layout of the pictures in *Little Pickle* provides a particular challenge for young readers. In the early pages there is a large central picture with two smaller ones at the top and bottom (illustration 3). The child's eye will certainly be drawn to this middle one first, but to get the events in sequence, the top-to-bottom, left-to-right convention has to be followed. Later in the same book other inventive formats are used to indicate the sequence of events.

Having learnt to follow a picture story from left to right, young children's ideas are extended by sequences such as breakfast time in *Sunshine*. Here two episodes are being played out simultaneously: the little girl eats her breakfast in the foreground while Dad, intent on his paper, burns the toast behind her. This caused problems for a group of three year olds, not of sequencing but of understanding. They had no idea that Dad was burning the toast; they interpreted the smoke-filled room as:

Imogen: *It's dark*
Teacher: *Why is it getting darker I wonder?*

Imogen: *Because he's switched the light off.*

The whole sequence that ends with Dad holding the burnt toast in his hand was incomprehensible to them, and yet there appears to be nothing particularly difficult about that idea or its representation. So it is important for an adult to be reading alongside the child.

The passing of time and the sequencing of events in wordless picture books are depicted in a variety of ways that children might not easily follow. Through a series of beautifully observed drawings in *Sunshine*, Jan Ormorod shows each stage the little girl goes through as she gets dressed. Each single picture has a red rectangle behind it, which both links

④

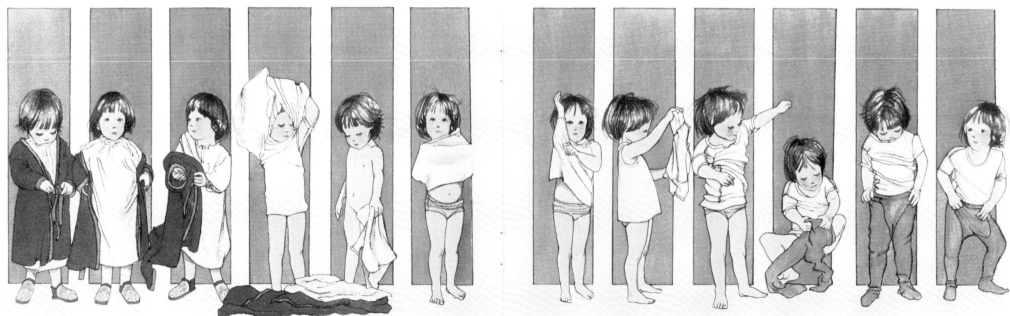

and separates them. This is not the usual box which contains an image, but a backdrop which defines the actions and indicates the sequential nature of the activity. However, to a three year-old it is not one little girl going through a sequence of actions in the process of dressing: it is 'lots of' little girls (illustration 4).

> Nicola: *There she's taking her vest off, there she's taking her vest off ... And she's got her trousers on and she's got her trousers on.*

Her emphasis on pronouns when telling this part of the story indicated that Nicola thought they were different girls. Her teacher sought to clarify her understanding:

> Teacher: *Is it one little girl or lots of little girls?*
>
> Nicola: *Lots of little girls.*
>
> Imogen: *Lots of big girls.*

An interesting parallel to the toast-burning sequence occurs in *Up and Up*. Again there are two events happening simultaneous in the same series of pictures. The little girl has landed on a roof and is being pulled off the TV aerial by the man in the balloon, while X-ray pictures show the effect of her contact with the aerial on the image on the TV of the man and woman below (illustration 5). The reader is called on to recognise the simultaneous nature of the events and also cause and effect.

There are two other examples in *Up and Up* of conventional graphic devices which might puzzle young children: seeing stars after a bump on the head, and the lines (dotted, double, multiple or spiral) indicating movement (illustration 6).

In *Little Pickle* readers are introduced to the 'bubble', indicating that the child in the pushchair is dreaming (illustration 7). The next four pictures have wavy lines around them, almost as if the illustrator is giving the reader time to absorb this information before reverting to the straight edges. Most four year olds will probably not have enough print experience to understand this convention. Katie's logical explanation for Mum being in the pushchair was that the little girl had got out and Mum had got in. However, after it was explained to her, she incorporated her new knowledge into her re-telling of the story to another child:

> Katie: *And they're going over the bridge to the park and she's having a dream about pretending her mummy is her and the little girl's the mummy.*

The Gift tells a story in a simple way but one picture might cause difficulties. Again this is to do with the depiction of an imaginary as opposed to a 'real' event. Towards the end of the adventure in the jungle, there appears above the heads of the two children a disproportionately small house, with food and drink in front of it (illustration 8). It would be obvious to an adult that this was a vision conjured up in the minds of the homesick children. This imaginative projection is not contained, as might be expected, in a 'bubble' but is instead given significance by a white background which contrasts with the green jungle.

The creative ways in which the illustrators of wordless picture books develop their stories means that young children might not extract the full meaning from them without some help. They have the visual and intellectual skills to understand the story but need an adult to focus their attention on certain information provided in the illustrations. They might also need help with conventions that we take for granted and which are vital to the meaning of the book, and which exploit the possibilities for complex narrative inherent in images. We explore this further in the following chapters.

References

Lewis, D. (1990) The Constructedness of Texts: Picture Books and the Metafictive. *Signal* Number 62, p.131-146.

CHAPTER 2

Things aren't always what they seem: introducing text

The way we normally speak of 'learning to read' disguises from us the fact that as children learn how to read they are also learning what reading is. Picture-book makers are clearly alert to this fact — that for their primary audience little needs to be taken for granted — and respond with displays of fluid invention that writers of prose narrative for older, more experienced readers find hard to match.

(Lewis 1990 p.143).

When print is introduced into picture books, it is usually in the conventional left-to-right mode under the picture. There are however, books which introduce text as an integral part of the image; it functions as part of the visual message rather than as parallel commentary. Words and pictures are interactive and the position of the words is crucial to their meaning. This can enhance the meaning of the story but it can be a problem for children who are just becoming familiar with the left to right convention. In the Meg and Mog books, for example, the text is arranged so that the meaning is enhanced by its proximity to the picture or by layout or comic-style graphics (illustration 9). These books use the printed word within the illustrations in a very arresting manner: labels, sound effects, speech and narrative appear all over the pages, enhancing meaning, extending the richness of the language experience of children and adding to the fun.

Another style of picture-book incorporates the now-popular convention of speech bubbles, which allows the author/illustrator to develop the story without long, complicated text. One book that uses this technique is *A Surprise for Oliver*. It exemplifies how a simple story can be extended and deepened by skilfully blending talk with pictures. Each page is packed with children busy doing all the things young children do in a nursery, inviting the reader to look carefully at the familiar events depicted. The text tells the story, but it is the children's talk which interprets the pictures for the reader while at the same time unifying the picture by showing that the apparently disparate activities are in fact connected (illustration 10). The quality of the talk also heightens the emotional response to the story and helps to convey directly and simply to the young reader, in a way that narrative text could not, the feelings aroused when a beloved toy is lost (illustration 11). The reciprocity between text and picture enables the child to enter more fully into the experience of the story — a vital aspect of becoming a reader.

Speech bubbles can not only extend the narrative as in *A Surprise for Oliver* but also provide contrast or contradiction, emphasising a different point of view. This allows children to be introduced early on to the idea of a dual reality in an accessible way. The economy and simplicity of this convention allows quite sophisticated concepts to be used, so that with adult help children can appreciate, for example, how Kevin's viewpoint differs from his family's in *The Perfect Day*. Here the main story is told in a simple, direct text. The bland style, almost parody, is set against the realism of Kevin's grumbles, with which children will readily identify, in the speech bubbles (illustration 12).

This dual representation of reality builds up page by page to the climax, where the roles are reversed and 'the perfect day' ends happily for Kevin — but not for the rest of the family!

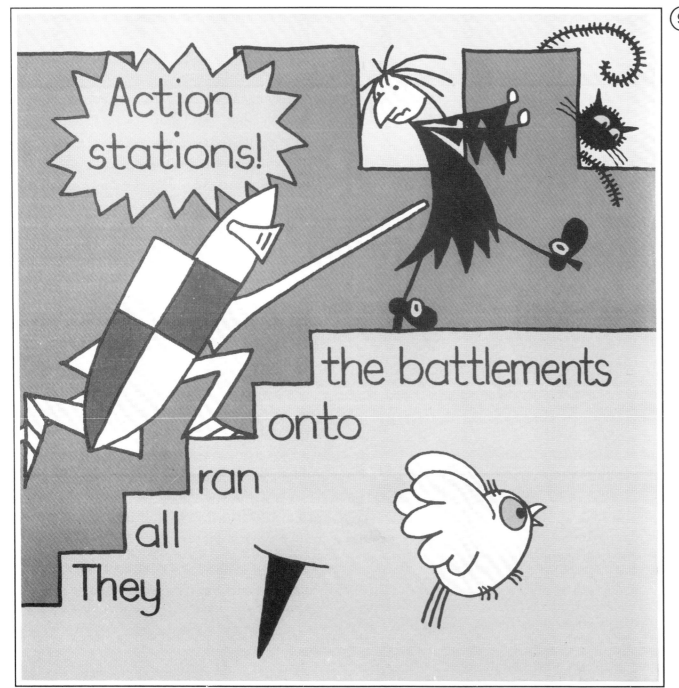

The dual viewpoint is explored rather differently in *Time to Get Out of the Bath, Shirley*, where domestic reality and the world of the child's imagination are juxtaposed. The pictures and text indicating Mum's perception of bath time present no problem. But the imaginary nature of Shirley's response is not indicated by text nor by conventional graphic means such as bubbles or wavy lines. Mum's nagging monologue is the only text, accompanied by pale, sparse drawings on the left-hand pages. It forces Shirley into a world of imagination on the right-hand pages that is colourful, richly textured, detailed and packed with action (illustration 13). The reader has to understand that the adventures Shirley has in her imagination are concurrent with Mum's actions and talk in the bathroom, possibly even precipitated by the boring reality of bathtime and Mum's automatic grumbling. It is the pictures which provide the contrasting viewpoint, while the text relating to reality emphasises and supports the pictures, so adding depth and humour to the story.

A further example of talk as narrative appears in *Never Satisfied*, a fascinating book, mysterious and challenging. Again, there is a conflict between text and image but here, as in *Rosie's Walk*, the reader has access in the pictures to events of which the characters appear unaware. The story is told through the comments of two boys, who are walking through an empty, stylised landscape complaining that they're bored because nothing ever happens. Behind them all sorts of weird and macabre events take place — a woman walks along a washing line to hang out her washing, while the boys say:

'No-one does anything different'.

The boys seem oblivious to the strange happenings — or are they? There are hints that perhaps they are not: a conspiratorial wink to the reader on the first page, a casual glance behind further on (illustration 14). What is the connection between the boys, their conversation and the surreal world they inhabit? This beautifully constructed story does not give up its meaning easily and both adult and child will find plenty to explore in the pictures and their links with the text.

It's a beautiful day, and there are lots of interesting places to explore.

These excellent picture books demonstrate that minimal text does not mean that the books are necessarily lightweight. In fact, the brief text can suggest layers of meaning through the skilful interaction of words and pictures, especially when the story is told in the words of the characters. The economy is a strength, not a limitation.

The understandings that children gain from exploring many-layered books with the help of an adult, will enable them to become readers in the real sense of the word, engaging with narrative at a far deeper level. By integrating speech into the picture the author can keep the narrative relatively simple, while introducing a new element which enhances the basic story. This might take the form of humour (*Meg & Mog*), introduce a personal, emotional element (*A Surprise for Oliver*), or it might depict another viewpoint (*The Perfect Day*). The notion of alternative views can be developed in other ways, such as contrasting text and pictures (*Never Satisfied*), or contrasting pictures (*Time to get out of the bath, Shirley*), and is an effective way of moving children towards an appreciation of subtext and irony. These books make visual what more sophis-

Now there's water everywhere!

ticated texts use language to imply, and they give children access to a device which deepens their appreciation of a story at a level they can understand. With sensitive intervention by an adult, children will become accustomed to searching for more than one meaning and realise that things are not always as they seem.

Reference

Lewis, D. (1990) The Constructedness of Texts: Picture Books and the Metafictive. *Signal* Number 62, p.131-146.

⑭

CHAPTER 3

Don't throw the picture books out with the Infants: developing responses

When parents and teachers share picture books with younger children, they are principally concerned with ensuring that the children understand what is happening and helping them to follow the sequence of events. If there is any discussion (children tend to want you to get on with the story!) it is usually of the sort that links the children's personal experience with the characters and events and occasionally predicts what might happen next. We believe that some picture books merit further exploration, and can be used to develop children's ability to reflect imaginatively on what they are reading and to deepen their understanding.

Sometimes however, younger children need to be thoroughly familiar with the book before they can begin to think about what is happening behind the story. Children might have shared *My Brother Sean,* for example, several times at home, in nursery or reception class. They will be familiar with the story of Sean crying when he is first taken into school but soon settling down happily. But they might not have talked about why, if Sean was so anxious to go to school in the first place, he suddenly started to cry when he got there! Nor might they have been asked what they thought helped Sean to settle into school. Similarly, children might have shared picture books like *Too Big* and *Rosie's Babies,* to help them come to terms with a new baby brother or sister or to explore feelings of 'jealousy'. They might not, however, have been asked why Harry opened Jake's box and put on Jake's clothes, or why Rosie started talking about *her* babies — nor why she later stopped talking about them. Or when exploring that feeling that grown-ups have a much more exciting time than they do, children might read *Why do Grown Ups have all the Fun?* But they might not be challenged to explore why Hannah decides to go back to bed even though she isn't told to (illustration 15).

Such questions open out possibilities for conversations about characters and events in picture books. Children can make greater links between their personal experiences and what they are reading than if all that is said is: 'You have a teddy like that, haven't you?', or 'We go to the park sometimes, don't we?', or 'We make sure that no one is on their own in the playground, don't we?' Questions should make imaginative demands on children, taking them beyond a superficial level of identification with the story towards the deeper level of thinking about people's motives. So for example, once the children are familiar with *Alex and Roy,* ask: 'Why doesn't Alex want to play with Roy?'. This might set them thinking about the front cover of the book, or the arrangements between Alex's mother and Roy's sister Renee, or the way that Alex appears to be playing on his own when the doorbell rings. A teacher might follow up by reading to page 8, where Alex's mother and Roy go to find Alex:

Together they peered into Alex's room.
Alex was sitting behind the door, looking very, very, very cross.
Only his mother saw him.

The children could think about what Alex's mother could do about him (illustration 16). Many picture books have this potential for promoting thoughtful discussion and imaginative responses. Even a deceptively straightforward book like *On Friday Something Funny Happened* offers considerable scope for discussion about whether or not the children in the story are being naughty (illustration 17). Young readers could imagine what the other people in the supermarket might be saying to or about the parents, or what Uncle John told a friend about his visit to the family (illustration 18). Such discussions would help enrich children's thinking about the centrally important issues: why were things different on Friday? and whether the two children in the story enjoyed Friday?

Other seemingly straightforward picture books, like *The Grass is Greener*, open up areas for discussion that go well beyond the scope of infants. While younger children could be asked what they thought about Lincoln at various stages in the story (e.g. 'Is Lincoln such a silly lamb, as one of the other lambs suggests?'), older children might consider how the other sheep might react to Thomas if he had another bright idea (e.g. 'Why should we allow ourselves to be sheared and give up all our lovely expensive

(16)

wool?'). Adults might ask themselves as well as older children such questions as: 'Who had the better time — Lincoln or the other sheep? Did the sheep benefit from their excursion? Who might

have written this book and for whom? (Look at the dedication at the back of the book.) What is the moral of this book and is it a laudable one?' Questions of this kind demonstrate the potential for developing children's thinking well beyond what could be expected of them at the level of Key Stages 1 and 2.

It is the power of certain picture books to stimulate interesting language work that makes us wonder why teachers of older primary children don't make more use of them. Teachers whom we have encouraged to use picture books report that they have no problems reading picture books with older children. If teachers are worried lest older children feel their dignity affronted, they can adopt certain strategies: they can ask the children to sift through a new collection of picture books and advise on their suitability for younger children, or to select for display and discussion the picture books that made greatest impact on them when they were younger.

Some picture books lend themselves to a problem-solving approach. For example, children could suggest solutions to Rosie's dilemma when her ice-cream supply runs out and Bill Coley refuses to help her until the end of the month[1]; or how the lighthouse keeper's wife could prevent the seagulls from eating her husband's lunch.[2] What could Bella do to get back Dogger for David?[3] What might Beatrice and Vanessa do when confronted by the wolves,[4] or Capillaris do to prevent Cousin

On Saturday we went shopping....

Blodwyn from taking her over completely?[5] Picture books like *To-day was a Terrible Day* and *Fourteen Rats and a Rat-Catcher* are admirable resources for supporting a programme designed to help children develop their narrative technique.

(19)

Being given endless stories to write during primary and early secondary school cannot be expected to improve children's skills in telling and writing stories. Concentrating instead on aspects of story-writing that they find difficult (e.g. ending a story) and giving them appropriate practice is more likely to develop their ability to shape narrative. So the teacher might read to page 20 of *Today was a Terrible Day*, then ask the children to discuss/write what they thought Miss Tyler had written in her note, and whether or not the note will end the story and why (illustration 19). Similarly with *Fourteen Rats and a Rat Catcher*, the teacher can stop at the vital moment when the rat catcher and the biggest rat go looking for each other in the barn, encouraging even the least able child to write or tell how the author will finish the story, judging from what they have heard so far. More able children might enjoy completing the story in the style of the dual narrative viewpoint which characterises this book.

Linking picture books can help nine to twelve year olds to think more deeply about the issues raised, especially if the children explain the links they or the teacher have made. *Today was a Terrible Day* has potential for discussion (e.g. 'Why might Rosemary be behaving in the way she did? What motivates people to read?') and could also be linked with, say, *I'll Take you to Mrs. Cole* and *The Not-so-Wicked Step-mother*, within a theme of Learning about Grown-ups (especially those about whom children might hold preconceived ideas). The actual note that Miss

Tyler wrote to Ronald revealed to him that she wasn't quite the ogre she seemed and was far more sensitive to Ronald's plight than he could possibly have imagined. Ironically (despite the Rockets reading book!) she managed to hit on the perfect way for him to realise that he could read. In *I'll take you to Mrs Cole* the children can be encouraged to appreciate Mrs Cole, who seems at first a night-marish figure, by imagining what it must be like for the boy when he returns home from school each day. 'Is he being naughty?' (illustration 20) 'Why doesn't the threat of punishment work?' 'Consider the differences between the boy's mother and Mrs Cole, and the way they live.' Older children could write a social worker's report on the suitability of the two households as homes for children, follow-ing police intervention to discover the boy's where-abouts after he's seen wandering the streets. Or they could write a report from the school in re-sponse to the police enquiry.

The Not-So-Wicked Stepmother deals with a poten-tially sensitive area for some children, so discussion needs to be centred on the characters in the book. It provides an excellent opportunity for developing awareness of subtext, which is crucial if children are to move towards a full appreciation of the book. *The Not-So-Wicked Stepmother* invites a variety of re-sponses and is a good example of a picture book suitable for a wide age range. Familiarity with the stereotype of the wicked stepmother is an obvious prerequisite, but at what age children should read this book will be for the adult to decide. Younger children might be asked questions designed to help them identify more closely with Hessie; older children would be encouraged to exercise their powers of empathy and consider the adults' feelings hinted at in the text and pictures. So, with younger children, the teacher might set the scene verbally and then ask how Hessie will feel when her mum suggests that she goes to stay with her dad for the summer. Older children might be asked what the mother felt as she packed Hessie's suitcase. Younger children could explore what Hessie's stepmother would be like, while older children could predict how Hessie's mother might respond if Hessie voiced her fears about her new stepmother. Younger children might discuss why Hessie reacted as she did over the shower, while older children think also about how Molly must have felt, and how she got through the rest of the day until Hessie's father returned. It would be important for young children to discuss how Hessie might be feeling as she says goodbye on the final page, and it would be valuable, though demanding, for older children to try to imagine the possible thoughts of Hessie's Dad and Molly. Examples of older primary children discussing this book can be found in the next chapter.

This capacity for empathy is important for picture books like *Piggy Book*, but it is not only empathy that makes this book rewarding for older children. Intentionally or unintentionally, it is not as clear-cut as it first appears. Children's thinking would need to be extended beyond noting the faded, sepia-like pictures of the almost faceless mother and the close-ups of the obnoxious father, to begin questioning how far the problems posed in this book are actually resolved (illustration 21). This is best done in stages.

So the readers would first identify the problems by asking questions like: 'What appear to be the father's attitudes and why? Why does the mother go out to work? Where might she have gone when she left them? Why did the family want her back? Why did she come back? Why is it assumed that the men won't be able to cope? Why not? What if the mother had stayed away a bit longer? What else was she doing besides repairing the car?' Questions of this nature might assist older children to reflect on just how satisfactory they find the book's ending.

The books discussed here deal with important human emotions and issues but do so with economy, leaving much implied in the subtext. Consequently, there is space for children to bring their experiences to bear on the meaning of the books, but unless the teacher helps them to do so much of that meaning will remain unrevealed.

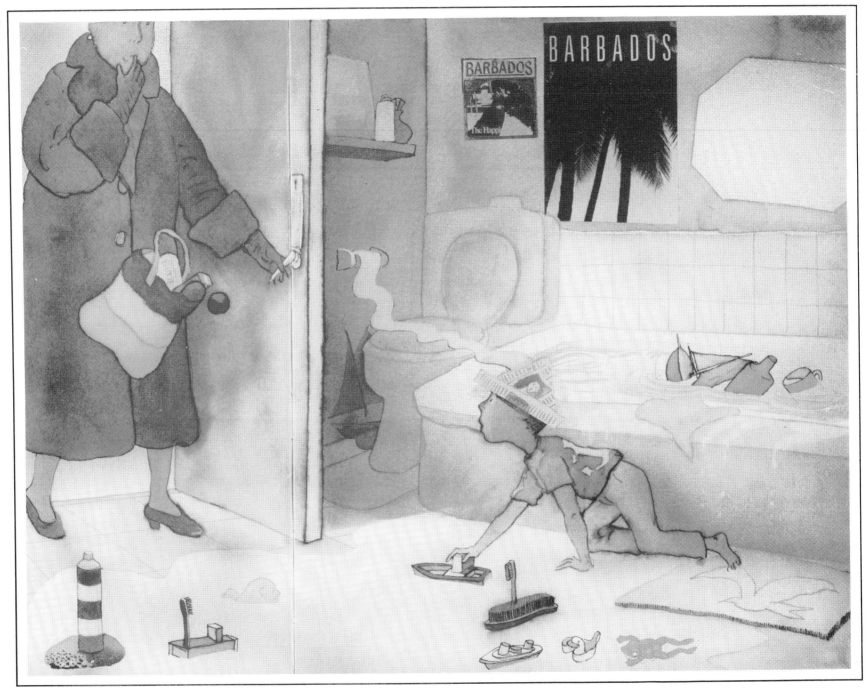

She mended the car.

㉑

References

1. *Ice Cream for Rosie* by Ronda and David Armitage, Hippo Books.

2. *The Lighthouse Keeper's Lunch* by Ronda and David Armitage, Andre Deutch.

3. *Dogger* by Shirley Hughes, Picture Lions.

4. *Beatrice and Vanessa* by John Yeoman and Quentin Blake, Macmillan Children's Books.

5. *Cousin Blodwyn's Visit* by A. Vesey, Methuen Children's Books.

CHAPTER 4

Playing around with the familiar: traditional tales and modern picture books

Fairy stories are part of most children's experience of literature. Most young children in the UK are familiar with *Cinderella, Red Riding Hood* and *Goldilocks*. The fact that different countries and cultures have stories in which the same elements occur indicates that certain themes have basic human appeal. Indeed, Jung sees the hero myth in which the prince sets out on a journey, gains his independence, kills a dragon, wins the beautiful princess and acquires his kingdom, as giving shape and artistic expression in literary form to a basic psychological experience. It is only recently that fairy stories have been regarded as merely for children.

Fairy stories deal with powerful human emotions that we all have to come to terms with in our lives: jealousy, insecurity, sibling rivalry, usurpation, feelings of inadequacy and the transforming power of love. Through fairy stories children are helped to accept and come to terms with their own feelings and those of others, much as great literature can illumine the lives of adults.

Certain aspects which are characteristic of many fairy stories may help this process. The setting of 'a long time ago' and 'in a far-off land' distances events and characters, making the often frightening episodes less threatening. The format whereby good always triumphs over evil, characters behave in predictable ways, expectations are realised and endings are always happy, gives a sense of security. The more bizarre parts of the plot are more readily accepted because there is a predictable pattern. 'Once upon a time' anticipates not only the prince, princess, giants and witches but also 'and they all lived happily ever after'.

Nathan
(7 years): *Fairy stories finish with a good ending.*

Ben
(10 years): *I think the most traditional thing that happened was when the woodcutter came along 'cos someone's got to save them and it's the same in Little Red Riding Hood — the woodcutter comes and saves them.*

Michelle
(10 years): *It's the same with all the films as well um you know um nothing's going ... they're not going to get killed um 'cos they're the goodies and they're the baddies and the baddies always get killed.*

Because the sometimes outdated and stylised language in traditional versions is strange to today's children it reinforces the sense of remoteness. At the same time, the predictability of style gives a sense of security. There are inversions ('so go they did'), archaic phrases ('wept bitterly', 'his joy was great') and repetition. These linguistic devices are as much a part of fairy stories as the beautiful youngest daughter and wicked stepmother. Fairy stories tend to have stereotypical characters, so children know where they are; there is good and bad and very little in between. Stepmothers are wicked, the youngest sibling tends to be good, kind, with moral courage and a forgiving nature. Boys are active and brave, girls passive and waiting to be rescued or awoken. This can be limiting for the young child in identifying with the characters, but the predictable nature of these stereotypes does provide a certain recognition and reliability.

One recent trend is to take a traditional story as a starting point and change it in some way. Alan Garner (1988) sees these variations as a threat to children, as 'false':

> Fairy tales are now commonly tinkered with for biased ends, and they are subverted by knowing cynics, to be used as vehicles for private wit.
> (Garner, 1988 p.8).

This seems to be a narrow and rather precious reaction. The fact that the tales have survived for so long and appear in different versions in different countries indicates that the form is robust enough to withstand changes. Provided that older children are familiar with the traditional tales, these reworked versions can even increase involvement and develop children's thinking about the story, because they invite comparison and are interesting in themselves.

There are many ways of changing fairy stories; we have chosen two reworkings to illustrate our argument. They employ totally different styles but in both cases children will need to be familiar with the traditional stories to appreciate fully the skill of the

author/illustrator. If children have recently revisited the traditional stories in conventionally illustrated versions (e.g. Susan Jeffers' *Hansel and Gretel* whose pictures support understanding of the text), they will be ready for the demands made upon them by an illustrator such as Anthony Browne, whose pictures expand the story in a thought-provoking way (illustration 22).

Michelle:	*I think there's a relation... I think the stepmother... that's her mother or something because she's got a spot like that.*
Ben:	*It's the witch.*
Michelle:	*... and she's got a spot like it... She's planned it that they should go to the house and she'd try and kill them or something and they'd (she and her husband) live happily ever after.* (Others join in and refer to other pictures for comparison)
Ben:	(Reflecting on previous page) *It's cleverly made with all the things exactly the same, the face and the spot.*
Ruth:	*That's why, that's why in the other book like she had the same top. That's why this book all explains the other book.*
Ben:	*Oh yeh, the other book it was the same woman then.* (At this point they give extra confirmation to the link they have made by remembering

that the witch and the stepmother both die at the end of the traditional story.)

Ruth:	*All these things when she's dead now... then all these things kind of like she could be trying to haunt them or she's meant to die when the old witch is pushed in the oven, the lady at home dies at exactly the same time when she's pushed in the oven.*
Ben:	*Like Indiana Jones and The Temple of Doom, they had this woman and she stabs her dolly.*
Michelle:	*I think they're the same.*
Ruth:	*They are.*
Ben:	*Yeh.*

Apparently, then, picture book versions of traditional tales allow children new ways to engage with and reflect upon the story. Ben commented spontaneously immediately after the conversation reported above:

> If you were just reading the story you wouldn't notice all the clever things like the wardrobe picture, the witch in that is the same, and there's little things that you wouldn't normally notice and the trees and the shapes of hands.

Anthony Browne's symbolic use of colour, shape and pattern in his version of *Hansel and Gretel* compels the reader to be constantly aware of the physical, emotional and spiritual dimensions of the story.

The children recognised the repeating patterns and they began to understand what the patterns referred to. They were also able to reflect on how the artist was helping them to interpret what the patterns meant (illustration 23). Ben had already begun to link the bar-like images with the idea of prison when Ruth said:

> It's like what Ben said, they're going further and further and the bars are getting bigger and they're going further and further into the bars and then in the end they are going into the bars.

Ben: *And at the beginning where it said 'published by' at the first page there's a bird in the cage and I think the person who wrote this book was pretty clever to think of that. I don't know why he did it 'cos not many people are going to notice it.*

Ruth: *The cage, the cage!! Gretel's going to be put in the cage.*

Such moments of insight happened not once but several times. The children's understanding deepened and they were able to internalise it — as the excitement in their voices proclaimed.

The following transcription shows how the quality of the illustrations, the nature of the teacher's intervention and the children's own literary experiences combined to enable them to grasp the symbolic nature of the images and appreciate the deeper meaning within the story (illustration 24).

(23)

Lisa:	*The trees have gone and also the doors are clean and the logs aren't the same.*
Ruth:	*It looks like they've had it done up.*
Ben:	*It's a sunny house and also that door is like the wardrobe with the mirror, that is exactly a mirror and that is the bottom of it.*
Teacher:	*My word, you're observant, and as Ruth has said there is a new seed growing. And why is it from the inside of the house? Why is the picture taken from the inside of the house?*
Ruth:	*There's a new leaf turning over.*
Teacher:	*Right, and what gives you that idea?*
Ruth:	*The seed.*
Teacher:	*The seed and what else?.*
Lisa:	*The trees and everything.*
Ben:	*The wardrobe, instead of there being a horrible... the door is the wardrobe, the bottom is exactly the same.*
Lisa:	*And it's much cleaner.*
Teacher:	*And which way are you looking?*
All:	*Outside.*
Teacher:	*You're all looking outside into the what?*
Ruth:	*The open air.*
Teacher:	*Into the open air and the light... yes, and all that horrible dark interior has disappeared.*
Ben:	*And they've passed out of the darkness into the light.*
Teacher:	*So they've come out of the what, then?*
Ben:	*Out of the dark.*
Teacher:	*Yes... I'm thinking of your idea....* (General interruptions)
Teacher:	*Hold on a moment, let's keep on Ben's idea.*
Ben:	*They're coming out of the cage aren't they?*
Lisa:	*I'll tell you something else as well, the bars have gone off the door.*
Michelle:	*Everything you really see her wearing are dark colours and when she's living there all the dark colours are around the house.* (She takes time to flick through the pages gathering evidence) *And when she's dead all of it becomes bright* (illustration 25).
Ben:	*She rules the world and the whole world is dark but now there's a rainbow to say she's gone.*
Teacher:	*Um.*
Lisa:	*There was one thing what she was hiding (jewels) 'cos they're light she kept that (the chest) shut because if she'd have opened it all the lightness would have come out.*
Teacher:	*Yes, because she's hoarding it all to herself, she's not sharing it and giving it out.*
Ben:	*Oh yes, so when the door's open all the light shines all over the world.*

| Ruth: | *And it's like Noah's Ark 'cos God sends a rainbow to say he'll never send a flood again, and there (pointing to picture of a rainbow) it says it'll never be dark again.* |

Fiona French's version of Snow White, *Snow White in New York*, tells the story through a very brief text and transposes it magnificently into art nouveau style illustrations. She retains the basic plot but changes details of the story to fit in with the new setting. Although the story is not fleshed out in any detail, the children were very evidently challenged by the ways Fiona French plays around with language in her version (illustration 26).

Michelle: What's 'classiest dame'? What's that supposed to mean?

Ben: Oh, in the 'New York Mirror', the paper, that's good that is.

Teacher: Yes, it is, but hold on a moment let's deal with Michelle's question first. What does it mean 'the classiest dame in New York?'

Michelle: She was the most popular person.

Ruth: The prettiest.

Michelle: But she isn't though!

Teacher: Classy doesn't only mean pretty and attractive.

Ben: She knows what to wear.

Michelle: It's like the chocolates 'A Touch of Class'.

All the papers said that Snow White's stepmother was the classiest dame in New York. But no one knew that she was the Queen of the Underworld. She liked to see herself in the New York Mirror.

Ben:	*She knows, I mean, what lipstick to put on, which goes with her make-up.*
Teacher:	*Yes, she's a good dresser.*
Michelle:	*That's a touch of class isn't it?*
Teacher:	*Yes.... what else does it mean if you're classy?*
Michelle:	*That you're beautiful....*
Lisa:	*Brilliant.*
Michelle:	*...know everything. Smart. Clever.*
Teacher:	*You know how to behave in certain ways.*
Lisa:	*Towards men.*

Because the children already knew the story, they had some idea of what 'classiest dame' might mean. They went on to help each other to tease out the subtleties embedded in the phrase, and came to a surer grasp of its meaning as a result of their teacher's persistent pressure to clarify and extend their ideas. The children were involved in similar discussions when trying to understand the phrases 'poor little rich girl' and 'Queen of the Underworld'. It is indicative of the challenging nature of Fiona French's style that most of these discussions were initiated by children's questions.

Before they were introduced to the Fiona French edition, the children were encouraged to think about modernising the story themselves. This helped them to explore the feelings and motivations of the characters in greater depth than they might have done from reading the traditional ver-

sion. Having already established that Snow White was fashion-conscious, in her tight jeans and leather jacket, the group's discussion of the step-mother begins to reveal their understanding of her behaviour towards Snow White. The teacher's role here appears to be to give back to the children their own ideas in a slightly different form:

Ben:	*The mother would try to be even more slick than Snow White.*
Teacher:	*So there's competition here between the mother and the daughter?*
Ruth:	*The father loves Snow White more. She (the Queen) wants him to love her more, so she dresses up too much but the King still loves Snow White more.*
Teacher:	*Ah, so there's jealousy about the father's thinking the daughter's more beautiful than the mother?*

When this group of children looked at *Little Red Riding Hood*, they again explored feelings and motivation, reversing the stereotypical role of the wolf, and presenting him in a more favourable light:

Little Red Riding Hood from the Wolf's Point of View

I remember that it was a beautiful warm sunny day and all I was doing was having a pleasant nap in the grass by the side of the path, when suddenly I was rudely awoken by that aggravating spoilt brat cheekily screeching at the top of her voice: 'Who's afraid of the Big Bad Wolf, the Big Bad Wolf?', etc.

But because she was so little and looked so nice in her new red hood I held my tongue and just spoke nicely to her, asking her if she needed any help because she appeared to have wandered off the main path and entered the darkest and most dangerous part of the forest. But she stuck her tongue out at me and very impolitely shouted at me to mind my own business and then ran off into the thickest part of the forest singing 'Who's afraid of the Big Bad Wolf'. Well, of course, I was very worried that she might get lost so I just had to go and warn her granny. (Ben, Lisa, Michelle, Ruth).

Modern versions of traditional stories can clearly revitalise older children's interest in the tales and develop their understanding of deeper layers of meaning. Children gain the confidence to reshape familiar material for themselves. Playing around with familiar material allowed the children further to explore character and motivation, and might have helped towards their using parody later. To conclude this chapter, we pick up our comment in the last: that children can develop their thinking by linking one picture book with another. In this case stepmothers were the link. The children progressed from the traditional portrayal of stepmothers in *Hansel and Gretel* and *Snow White* to a picture book that questions the stereotype — Lizi Boyd's *The Not-So-Wicked Stepmother*.

After reading *Hansel and Gretel* and *Snow White* the children could empathise with Hessie's view of stepmothers, and were more adept at interpreting pictures, text and symbolism. So they were better prepared to meet the rather different challenge — of reading the subtext in *The Not-so-Wicked Stepmother*. Lizi Boyd skilfully selects crucial moments of heightened emotion, such as when Hessie's belongings are packed for her trip to her dad; her first meeting with Molly and other key moments in the evolving relationship, culminating with the incident in the shower. Because there are a number of significant incidents, and because they are passed over without authorial comment, it is vital that the teacher encourage children to reflect at each stage on what might be going on under the surface (illustration 27).

| Teacher: | *I wonder what Mum might be feeling about Hessie going? What do you think?* |
| Ruth: | *She might be feeling lonely 'cos her husband has got someone but she hasn't, so she needs Hessie.* |

(27)

Lisa: *My Mum gets lonely without me, she usually talks to the dog.*

Teacher: *I wonder what Hessie's feeling about going away tomorrow?*

Ruth: *She knows her Mum's lonely so she wants to stay.*

Lisa: *Sick of everything, she just wishes her Mum and Dad... she thinks it's a nightmare.*

Hessie's own mother has not died (as in *Hansel and Gretel* or *Snow White*) and children need to come to terms with this. Hessie has her own mother as well as her stepmother to consider and this becomes increasingly important to her as the story progresses. As the stereotypical image of the wicked stepmother breaks down, Hessie is forced to start regarding Molly as an individual in her own right. This in turn undermines the neat barrier that safely separated Hessie's feelings about her mother from her feelings about her stepmother. Lizi Boyd is offering a modern adaptation rather than translation. In a translation the fact that the girl likes her stepmother would simply provide relief, whereas here it also creates tension.

Teacher: *But what about seeing her Dad?*

Lisa: *She's probably pleased to see her Dad but not very happy to leave her Mum.*

Teacher: *Yes, perhaps she's torn between the two, longing to see her Dad because she hasn't seen her Dad.....*

Lisa: *(interrupting) I'd hate to have to choose between my Mum and Dad, I wouldn't know who to go to.... and if you went with one person you'd hurt the other.*

thirty-nine

Teacher:	*Yeh, that makes it very difficult doesn't it?*

The children appear quite capable of seeing beneath the surface and understanding the feelings of both Hessie and her mother, and also Hessie's tension when she leaves her Mum to go to her Dad's. They also sympathise with Hessie's opinion of her stepmother; but the real challenge of the subtext of this book is to take the children beyond the stereotype to seeing Molly as an individual.

Teacher:	*I wonder about Molly? What might be going on in Molly's mind?*
Ruth:	*She probably thinks she's going to be a lovely adorable little child (laughing).*
Lisa:	*A nice little sweet kind of girl.*
Teacher:	*So she's looking forward to seeing Hessie?*
Lisa:	*Yeh, 'cos it's got it at the front — 'a really kind stepmother'.*
Teacher:	*So you think because of the title that Molly's looking forward to seeing Hessie?*
Ruth:	*She might not be looking forward to seeing her...*
Teacher:	(interrupting) *Why not?*
Ruth:	*.... she might be jealous.*
Teacher:	*Why are you saying that she might be jealous?*
Ruth:	*Because of the husband — he's got children and she hasn't.*

Teacher:	*Ah yes, that's an interesting idea. Now Lisa, what were you saying?*
Lisa:	*That she hasn't got children, so she's not looking forward to seeing Hessie because she wants her own children. She doesn't want her husband's child, she wants her own.*
Teacher:	*On the other hand, presumably she loves her new husband?*
Lisa:	*Yeh, she's probably going to like her stepdaughter, but she would prefer her own children.*
Teacher:	*Umm, that's interesting to think about the different points of view. I wonder what Hessie's Dad will be thinking?*
Ruth:	*He probably thinks they're going to get on really well but they're actually going to hate each other's guts!*
Teacher:	(laughing) *Alright, let's see what happens.*

Despite appearing to read the subtext, there are indications in this discussion that the children are still heavily influenced by the Hansel and Gretel/Snow White stereotype stepmother — who would be jealous and unwelcoming. The children, despite the contrary evidence of the text, continue, like Hessie, to suspect that there is malice lurking beneath Molly's apparent kindness.

Teacher:	(reading) *'Stepdaughters are not supposed to like their stepmothers'.*

What does that tell us about Hessie and Molly and their relationship?

Ruth: *She's getting to like her.*

Teacher: *Why is she worried about that — getting to like her stepmother?*

Lisa: *Just in case she got to like her and then she starts being really horrible.*

But by the time they reach the point where Dad goes back to work, the children seem to be persuaded by Molly's behaviour that she is not, after all, a stereotypical stepmother.

Teacher: *(reading) 'Now maybe Molly will be the mean stepmother'.*

Ruth: *She's going to be really kind to her 'cos it's kind of like her Mum and Dad leaving her with a stranger.*

Consequently they have no difficulty in empathising with Molly over Hessie's outburst when shampoo gets in her eyes in the shower (illustration 28).

Teacher: *(Reading) 'Mummy never washes my hair in the shower! You hurt me! I think you are wicked and mean!' I wonder what Molly will be feeling at that moment?*

Lisa: *Upset.*

Ruth: *Really upset.*

Teacher: *Um... can you talk a bit about that?*

Lisa: *She'd be feeling really hurt because she's been trying to be nice to her, then Hessie treats her like that. She's taught her to swim, she lets*

her feed the ducks, she's took her a
picnic to pick berries, then she acts
like that. It isn't really fair on
Molly.

Ruth: *She's made like a special arrange-*
ment to do everything with Hessie
while she's there.

Such empathy for Molly probably accounts for the
children's somewhat insensitive suggestions about
how Molly should react to Hessie's outburst.

Teacher: (Reading) *'Hessie cried and*
screamed until her Daddy came
home'.

I wonder what Molly did? I won-
der what you would have done if
you were Molly in that situation?

Lisa: *I wouldn't have done anything, I*
would have just left her.

Ruth: *I'd tell her to pack it in ... well, I*
wouldn't tell her to pack it in, after
a while I'd have got a headache, I'd
get all paddy and tell her to shut
up.

Although the children show greater sympathy with
Molly, it seems from their comments that they have
difficulty expressing understanding about the way
that Molly's feelings towards Hessie are affected by
her love for Hessie's Dad. This is evident from their
final discussion, when they talk about the end of the
book, where Hessie leaves her Dad and Molly to
return to her Mum (illustration 29). The teacher had
to ask the children repeatedly to consider Molly's

(29)

thoughts about Dad's feelings. Ultimately, though, they show much greater understanding of the complexities of Molly's reactions — indicating how far their thinking has progressed during the sharing of this book.

Teacher: *I wonder what's going on in Molly's mind?*

Lisa: *Be thinking that I'm really pleased that in the end we got on.*

Teacher: *Yes, kind of relief in a way that at least we've got on and that it's all going to be OK. What else might she be feeling given what you've said is going on in those people's minds?*

Ruth: *Sad, because she's kind of like been her Mum for six weeks.*

Teacher: *Yes, she's going to miss Hessie as well, so there's mixed feelings there. What might Molly be thinking about what is going on in Dad's mind?*

Ruth: *Kind of sad to leave.*

Lisa: *She probably doesn't want Hessie to go and she'll be pleased to see her again.*

Teacher: *Yes, she probably doesn't want Hessie to go and she'll be pleased to see Hessie again, but what do you think Molly is thinking about what Dad is feeling?*

Ruth: *She's going to be really sad to leave her Dad.*

Teacher: *Yes, but I'm not talking about Hessie, I'm talking about Molly and Dad. What do you think Molly will be thinking about what Dad is feeling?*

Lisa: *They are, they're probably going to be sad that she's going but also pleased that they can have some time to themselves.*

Teacher: *Right, they might feel a sense of relief that now they can have some time to themselves again.*

Lisa: *But sad that Hessie was going because she's been really nice.*

Teacher: *And what will Molly know that Dad will be feeling?*

Lisa: *Sad, he'll definitely be sad so Molly is going to try to be nice to him.*

Although the children didn't appear to be responding to the subtext spontaneously, they were obviously well able to read it when prompted. The very nature of picture books, with their interplay between text and picture and their economic use of text can, over a period of time, give the teacher an opportunity to develop children's awareness of subtext.

Picture books, then, can encourage children to use pictures to extend their understanding of the written text, to reflect on the meaning of language, to anticipate parody, to be aware of symbolism, to refer to other experiences — both literary and personal — in support of their ideas and, through the reading of the subtext, to move beyond stereotypical responses.

Reference

Garner, A. (1988) *Book of British Fairy Tales*. Collins.

CHAPTER 5

'Caring's about loving them and stuff': developing discussion

One of the important advantages for older children of working with picture books is that the brevity of text allows swift comprehension and overview that they seldom achieve when they read novels. That overview enables them to discuss the books in, arguably, a more sophisticated and satisfying way. For useful discussion to develop, a great deal will obviously depend on the quality of the book itself, but the teacher's questions are also important. A book like *Not Now Bernard* has the immediacy of impact and humorous quality to catch most children's attention. Guided by two questions from the teacher, a group of ten-year olds were led to engage with the text in a way that they might not have done with a lesser book. After reading the book to the whole class, the teacher told the group that he would be very interested to know what they thought of it; he also said that if he stayed for the discussion he would probably ask them whether there really was a monster in the garden, and whether they thought Bernard's parents cared for him. He then left them for twelve minutes to talk about their impressions of the book and perhaps come to some conclusions. (The transcript of the children's discussion and the one with the teacher when he returned, can be found in the appendix.)

Although there seemed to be general agreement that Bernard was simply pretending that there was this monster in the garden:

1. Harry: *I don't reckon there is a monster... he's just making it up sort of thing*

... what is more noteworthy is how the children constantly refer to the text, using it to support their ideas. Note also that this group is still operating at the stage where 'those who shout loudest win' — though Harry shows remarkable persistence!

47. Kate: *Yeh the monster is Bernard because the monster wouldn't know like how, what you're meant to do with the TV, what you're meant to do with a comic ....(interruption)*

50. Harry: *What it proves is... (interruptions) what it proves is ....(more interruptions) what it proves is ....(yet more interruptions) — she might have changed her clothes or something — no but what it proves is that he might as well be a monster, his parents wouldn't know the difference.*

That comment received initial approval from Kate but she re-thought her position almost immediately — a significant moment in the learning process and one which is perhaps more the product of pupil-to-pupil talk than teacher-pupil talk:

55. Kate: *......they just don't care....well I suppose they do care but they're just too busy with other things.*

This brought a swift riposte from Harry who points to the picture where Bernard's dad is sitting reading a newspaper and says:

58. Harry: *Well he's hardly been too busy with other things and stuff is he?*
(illustration 30)

That is the point in the conversation which gives rise to opposing viewpoints, an important ingredient for learning. Kate argued that Bernard's parents really did care for him but were too busy to be able to show him so, while Harry argued that Bernard's parents did not care for him at all. The quality of the book allows for such subtleties to be taken up by the children. It shows how some children will pick up such ambiguities in the text, while others might rely on the teacher to raise them, playing devil's advocate. Harry's profile suggested he was in the latter category, yet at times his contributions suggest he is approaching levels of attainment well beyond those expected for ten-year-olds.

Linking what is being read with personal experience is crucial to locking a reader into a text. We see it in this discussion — in the less inhibiting atmosphere of pupil-to-pupil discussion, that allows for argument, much re-reading of text and constant interruptions. Initially, the linking appeared to encourage thinking at the level of the particular:

65. Rebecca: *....and how could a monster read?*
66. Harry: *No, he's just looking at the pictures.... that's what I used to do when I was little.*

A little later, however, Kate and Rebecca appear able to generalise from their personal experience:

99. Harry:	*.....look, it says 'There's a monster in the garden and its going to eat me, said Bernard', and then it says 'Not now, Bernard'... so that's...he's just trying to get..he* (interrupted)
102. Kate:	*A proper, a really caring Mum and Dad would go along with it and imagine it was there.*
104. Harry:	*Yeh, they'd make a joke of it.*
105. Rebecca:	*Yeh, yeh* (interruptions) *'Is there really?! Oh, gosh!'*
106. Kate:	*Yeh, they'd go 'Is there really?! I bet you'd better stay indoors' or something like that.*

Not only does this illustrate how children can support and refine each other's statements (far less common in teacher-led discussions) but it also indicates their ability to move towards empathising and raising moral issues:

117. Kate:	*'Cos I mean if they didn't really, if they didn't really care they wouldn't even have any toys like that would they?*
119. Harry:	*No, I mean that isn't caring, they just say to him 'Here's some money, go out and get some toys'... they couldn't be bothered.....*

Despite Harry's domination of the discussion and forceful presentation of his opinions, he listened with care and understanding to a point Kate made earlier. He acknowledged its validity even though he disagreed with the main thrust of her argument concerning Bernard's parents. Furthermore, his comment indicates the degree to which he was able to empathise and consequently see himself in some kind of perspective, and the insight of his contribution was underlined by the amusing and highly appropriate voice he adopted for the young child and the parent:

121. Harry:	*No, but Kate's, Kate's right when she said that..you're right when you said that — what did you say, you said um...about a good parent would go along with it, I mean now at our age if I said to my mum that there's a monster in the garden she'd just ignore me because she'd think that I was just being stupid, but at that age five or six you'd go along with it....four or three you'd say 'There's a monster in the garden and it's going to eat me up' and you'd say 'Oh no! I'll go and get a gun and blow its head off!'*

Extending the discussion when the teacher rejoins the group or through a general feed-back session seems valuable — providing that interest is maintained. It allows for the development of ideas, which rarely happens in the conversation of a group of children left on their own, though an argument can help — as it did here. By focusing the group's attention on the pages where Bernard's mother prepares a meal for him and puts it by the television, the teacher was urging Harry to articulate in greater detail his view that Bernard's parents did not care for him (illustration 31):

165. Teacher: *.....Why do you think I was showing you those pictures?....*

168. Rebecca: *.....'cos the mother's making food for him.*

169. Kate: *If they didn't care they wouldn't bother about making food for him...*

171. Harry: *No, but they have to make food for him, I mean they've got to make food for him they can't just, it doesn't mean it doesn't mean they care if they make food for them or give them toys, caring's about loving them and stuff not just giving them toys and giving them food (interrupted)... and going along with his little jokes.*

A cross-curricular theme — personal relationships / parental care — had arisen quite naturally from a seemingly simple but actually rich context of a good picture book. Harry was making a sophisticated moral judgement and operating just then at a very sophisticated level.

The teacher might also contribute by manoeuvring the group towards considering new points of view. This one deliberately misunderstood what Hannah was saying in order to make the group think more deeply about Bernard's parents:

177. Hannah: *...and he smashed that up because he was so angry that no-one was taking any notice of him.*

179. Teacher: *Yeh... is Bernard, is Bernard a monster?*

Hannah did not appear to catch the teacher's meaning, whereas Harry did and cleverly refuted the suggestion by using it to reinforce his opinion of Bernard's parents. Partly to challenge Harry further and partly to make the others consider the possibility, the teacher pointed to the picture where Bernard says hello to his dad just as his dad is about to hammer a nail into the wall. He then drew their attention to the picture where Bernard says hello to his mum just as she is balancing on a stool to put something into the kitchen cupboard. His bid for closer observation of what was actually going on in the pictures failed to make any impression on Kevin's thinking! It confirmed Kate and Hannah's original opinions, since they regarded it as pure coincidence that Bernard spoke at those moments, but it did cause Harry to shift his position a little — which he was willing to admit publicly:

205. Harry: *Yes, as soon as his dad's hitting a nail in — yeh look at his eyes, his eyes are watching ....(interrupted) no, I don't reckon now ....(interrupted) I think I've changed, I've changed.*

208. Kate: *He didn't just think 'Oh, I'll make my Dad hit his finger with the hammer', he just, he just did it by accident.*

209. Harry: *No, I don't reckon.*

Those are important moments in the learning process, in terms of both a shift in thinking and of group dynamics. It takes courage at that age to admit to your peers that you are changing your mind in the light of fresh evidence. The teacher's presence allows such moments to be held up for inspection. After looking at the picture of Bernard with his dad, Kevin, Hannah and Kate expressed one opinion and Harry another, so the teacher intervened, to give them a momentary pause before making them weigh their opinions against the next piece of evidence:

210. Teacher: *Alright, now that's the conclusion you've come to.... look at the moment he's chosen to ask his mother.*

A little further on in the conversation the teacher attempted, with less than scintillating clarity, to summarise for Harry and the others the way in which Harry appeared to be changing his mind:

123. Teacher: *Harry's beginning to change his mind I notice....It's because Bernard's ignored that he's wanting to do things on purpose for a laugh, whereas before Harry was saying no, he was innocent.*

Giving space for summarising, allowing time for seeing the implications of a particular point of view and for reflection, are skills that are not easy to encourage in group discussions. Yet they are vital if children are to develop their thinking.

When present in the latter stages of a discussion the teacher may give children experience of such skills, so that gradually over time they begin to incorporate them into their own group discussions. Allowing children to listen to the tapes of their discussions and inviting them to comment on how they were helping each other to learn, can also help ensure a carry-over of skills. In addition, it will involve children in the whole business of assessment. The lesson Harry learned from this discussion may have been effectively internalised, partly because he made the judgement about his performance himself and partly because that judgement was tempered by the wider perspective of one of his peers and his teacher:

Teacher: *Harry, did you find it easy to work in that group?*

Harry: *Yeh, well sort of because it wasn't hard and it wasn't easy, you had to get your points over, you shouted a lot so they'd listen.*

Teacher: *Rebecca, how useful was it having Harry in the group?*

Rebecca: *Well, he gave a lot of the ideas or gave some of the ideas and we just gradually put more and more onto them. Well, he was the one who started us off really.*

Harry: *I just rabbit on and don't listen to anyone else and just say my point.*

Teacher: *Maybe that's something you need to learn about yourself, but certainly I would agree with Rebecca*

that you were the one who started things, you were the one who gave ideas and you were the one who also argued a point of view and supported it. You didn't just say it, you developed the idea, so there were some very useful things going on there.

Harry's judgement of himself is fair up to a point but errs on the negative side. This is typical of early judgements that individual children make of themselves. He needed the more positive aspects of his ability to be emphasised as well, so that he did not go into the next discussion feeling that he should keep his mouth shut. In fact he listened to other people's contributions more than he gave himself credit for, as demonstrated by his reference (121) to what Kate had previously said (102). It also illustrated some of the qualities that might be expected of a group leader: an ability to bring the conversation back to the point, to refer to someone else in the group, and to support that person by further developing what they said.

Kate must have felt a valued member of the group at that moment, but she (an 'able' child) must also have felt challenged to think harder by Harry's ability to argue against her using the evidence of the book (58) and the weight of a philosophical point (171). There is more one could say about Harry's contribution to this discussion, but the reality of classroom teaching would allow time for only the briefest profiling notes, perhaps with a reference to his having operated, at least twice, at a level well above that expected in standardised assessment of ten-year-olds.

When asked what she had learned about herself from listening to the tape, Rebecca's response was interesting for its group perspective:

Rebecca: *Well, next time we do it work out one problem at a time because we had too many questions that needed answers all at the same time, and we were getting a bit confused on which to do first.*

That prompted the teacher to ask the group about how they saw the role of the teacher in the discussion (something they had obviously not thought about). He suggested that next time they might take on the responsibility of pausing at some point in the course of their discussion to reflect on what had been said so far.

All this had been generated by sharing a picture book — one that contained complex ideas capable of being interpreted in a variety of ways.

CHAPTER 6

'Lurking in the bushes': encouraging a feel for language

Continuing the shared reading of picture books with 9 to 12 year olds significantly contributes to children's growing awareness of language, as they view the books through more experienced eyes and discuss them from different angles.

For younger children that early awareness of the potential of language appears to arise through humour, and especially rhyme. Picture books like *Don't Forget the Bacon*, *The Surprise Party* and *Naughty Nigel* deliberately play on the confusion arising from words that sound the same but mean totally different things. Although younger children are able to appreciate such humour, the challenge to play around with language better fits the capabilities of older children. They may well give it a try, especially if they are attempting to write something that will amuse children younger than they.

The rabbit's deliberate misunderstanding of the way the little girl in *Mr Rabbit and the Lovely Present* uses the word 'red' is a teasing play on the word:

'She likes red', said the little girl.
'Red', said Mr. Rabbit 'You can't give her red.'

This is subtle stuff, and might pass over the heads of infants and be better appreciated by older children. Similarly, older children will respond better to the way in which John Burningham plays with double meanings of certain phrases in *Mr Gumpy's Outing*. For example, Mr Gumpy allows animals to come on board his boat, providing that the pig doesn't 'muck about' and the hens 'don't flap.'

> Teacher: *Incidentally, why did you find that particularly amusing? I know you didn't roar with laughter but you seemed amused by it, why?*
>
> Jonathan (11): *'Cos pigs roll in mud ... muck ... in other words mud is like muck so .... and they're meaning it in the way 'don't be silly' but we're seeing it in a different way.*

Children's awareness of how language can be made to work is facilitated by discussing particular words pointed up by a writer in the course of a story. For example, in *The Angel and the Wild Animal*:

And sometimes the wild animal makes everyone WILD.

The deliberate play on alternative meanings of 'wild' might be obvious enough for young children to enjoy but gives older readers also the pleasurable realisation of what the author is up to. Immediate exploration of what 'wild' could mean might prompt such responses as 'very cross', 'extremely angry', 'exceptionally annoyed', 'furious', 'right out of control' etc. These responses are amusing and relevant to children because of both the context and the emphasis on the superlative. That emphasis could be further explored through improvisation.

A less immediately obvious, so perhaps more thought-provoking, play on words occurs in *On*

On Saturday we went shopping.

Friday Something Funny Happened. On the first page the children's escapade in the supermarket underlines the ironic use of the word 'shopping' (illustration 32). Later in the book, asking what the 'funny' thing that happens on the crucial day of the week is (and why) stimulates consideration of what the author means by the word 'funny' (illustration 33).

Teacher:	*What's the word that sticks out in your mind?*
Gareth (11):	*Funny, because that isn't funny.*
Jonathan (11):	*Funny, because they're strange. You could change funny to different but it wouldn't seem as...*

On Friday something funny happened— and the house was very quiet.

Gareth:	*Something different happened....*	Teacher:	*To different or strange ... anything else?*
Jonathan:	*But it wouldn't seem as...I don't know ...yeh*	Jamie (11):	*Weird.*
Teacher:	*So you could change the word funny...*	Teacher:	*Something weird happened.*
Ben (10):	*To different.*	Jonathan:	*Extraordinary.*
		Teacher:	*But why would you use the word weird? I know what you mean, but*

*why would you use the word weird
in this context?*

Jonathan: *'Cos that's never really happened
before* (laughter) *they've always
been messing around!*
(laughter)

Teacher: (laughing) *Yes!*

Ben: *And you can't expect four year olds
to do that.*

This discussion led the children to try using language in a similar way. Jamie, in the role of Uncle John (who visited the family on Tuesday), called the children's mother to thank her for lunch and said

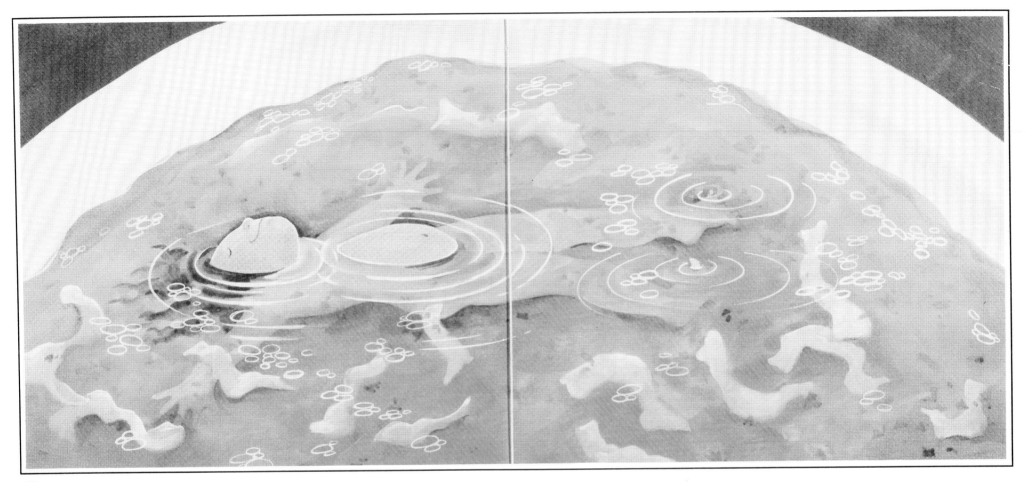

how he 'missed' the children. Jessica (11), wrote a brief 'thank you' note from Uncle John saying:

> Dear Valerie,
> Just a note to say thanks for inviting me. It was an unexpected delight so relaxing and enjoyable. Sam and Denise are wonderful children...

(illustration 34)

Playing with language to say something you don't quite mean for special emphasis — a tongue-in-cheek style — will probably be new and challenging for older children.

They might well begin to attune themselves to the ironic as they get older through becoming aware of the tone of voice required. For example, in *The Perfect Day*, the smooth, unruffled tone of the newscaster-type voice reporting the general scene is amusingly punctuated by Kevin's complaints, which suggest his world is anything but smooth and unruffled. It is the deliberate juxtaposition of two voices that indicates to the children (who have no problem with Kevin's tone of voice) how the narrator's voice must be interpreted. Similarly, in *Lucy says No*, Lucy's statements are themselves demanding but, as they are doubtless familiar to children reading the book, they do not present quite the challenge that the language and tone of voice of the other characters do. On page 4 for example, there are several ways in which the mother might say 'We'll just have the bread, then'. Experimenting with how she might say 'Come on, sunbeam' helps alert children to the power of irony. This in turn prepares children for the challenge of interpreting the way in which Lucy herself says 'See you in the morning' to the by now excommunicated doll, Pamela. Is her tone smugly self-satisfied or aggressively 'that's that'? Or is Lucy caught by the writer as she imitates her mother's ironic tone in a singsong 'See you in the morning'?

Children's growing awareness of language can be developed further by exploring the use of simile and metaphor in picture books. Again, it will be the amusing combination of text and picture that points up these powerful uses of language. In *A Difficult Day*, Eugenie Fernandes not only says of Melinda as she wallows in a gloriously warm bath that 'she felt like a noodle floating in a bowl of chicken soup', but actually portrays Melinda floating in a bath of

Mum laughed softly and Lucy listened
to her footsteps all the way down the stairs.
But she still felt angry inside,
so she took Pamela and went to the window.

A gentle breeze drifted through the crack.
Lucy wedged Pamela's soft body through
the opening and then gave her a whack.
Pamela went flying out into the quiet night.

"See you in the morning," said Lucy,
and climbed into bed.

(37)

soup (illustration 35). When finally made to get out of the bath, Melinda looks extremely flushed and crinkled from spending so long in the water. Her mother tells her that she looks like a prune, to which Melinda angrily retorts 'I *am* a prune'. The transformation from simile to metaphor has been simply and realistically accomplished within the text, so the reader is prepared for the next line 'Melinda, the prune, was sent to her room'. This metaphor echoes the description of James's classmates in *Just Awful*, when James has to wait in the nurse's room and

finds himself sitting next to 'a stomach-ache and a sore toe' (illustration 36). Even if children do not quite grasp the implications of: 'He sat down next to a stomach-ache and a sore toe', they are likely to realise what the writer is up to when she goes on: '*The* stomach-ache went in to see the nurse. James was left with *the* sore toe'.

Picture books can also encourage children to develop sensitivity to the uses of language for descriptive purposes. In *Francie's Day in Bed*, Francie stays home from school because her throat is 'scratchy'. Children will have experienced all kinds of discomfort associated with having a 'sore throat', but are likely to recognise just how Francie's 'scratchy' throat feels. The relief at not having to go to school, but also a certain sense of isolation at being alone in her bedroom while the family go about their normal daily routine, is well caught. Francie's main link with the rest of the world is through sound. Even the cat, although in Francie's room, is heard and not seen: 'the cat made a rumbling sound'.

This picture book stimulated a discussion amongst a class of 8 and 9 year olds over the distinction between being a bit poorly like Francie and being *really* ill as many of them had been at some time. James (8), who suffered badly from hay-fever, vividly described a particularly nasty attack while playing on the school field:

> Five minutes later my eyes were stinging so badly that I was half crying and then they burst, and I couldn't see a thing, it was like a thousand wasps stinging my eyes.

Bringing her own experience to the discussion about Francie's illness enabled James to capture his suffering in powerfully evocative language (no mention had been made of simile or metaphor).

In *Lucy Says No*, Maryann Macdonald describes feelings which children will surely recognise and which will help them engage with the precise and emotionally charged language on page 18:

> A gentle breeze drifted through the crack. Lucy wedged Pamela's soft body through the opening and then gave her a whack. Pamela went flying out into the quiet night.

The fun of the word 'whack', and its appropriateness in capturing Lucy's feelings while also describing what she actually does to the doll is worth drawing attention to, and its violent contrast with the 'gentle breeze', as Pamela's 'soft body' is sent hurtling into the peacefulness of the night (illustration 37).

Teacher: *So you've got this nice gentle breeze, the soft body of the doll and the pleasantly quiet night outside and what is the word .... just as Cathy* (referring to the way Cathy had acted out the part of Lucy)...

Martin (10): *Whacked.*

Teacher: *Yes, now why should that be funny and amusing?*

Jonathan: *Because everything else is all gentle and nice and soft and then suddenly there's this very strong word.*

There are a number of ways in which the teacher could help children to appreciate Maryann Macdonald's choice of simple yet powerful words. The children might be invited to act the part of Lucy waiting for her mother to disappear downstairs. Or to be Dad having a quiet beer in the garden when Pamela is rocketed out of the bedroom window. Or they might take the part of others in the family spying Pamela in the flower bed next morning; or the nextdoor neighbour bringing her back.

Cathy: *Oh I'm sorry to bother you but I found this doll lurking in my bushes — is it yours?* (The children laugh)

Teacher: *Yes, I loved the way you used the word lurking* (more laughter). *There's an example of Cathy using language in an ironic way because she ...she... why is it ironic, why is it amusing?*

Ruth (10): *It's funny because you don't expect to find a doll lurking in the bushes.*

Jonathan: *Because lurking is something you'd use for something that's alive and a doll isn't really alive.*

Teacher: *Yes, and who might lurk?*

Vicky (11): *Prowlers, burglars.*

Ruth: *Foxes.*

Teacher: *Yes, a stealthy animal like a fox which is creeping up on its prey, or burglars, or criminals of some sort lurking around — it's not a pleasant word is it and yet...*

Vicky: *We laughed.*

Teacher: *Yes* (laughing) *and Cathy played around with the idea that there's this neighbour who's terribly scared because of this doll lurking in the bushes* (laughter) *— so it's a lovely use of language because the neighbour knows only too well whose doll it is.*

Martin: *Yeh, and she's trying to be funny.*

Unless children are consciously encouraged to pay attention to detail they might not learn to appreciate ways in which language can be employed for effect. If this is done sensitively and without labouring the point, a good picture book like this one offers an ideal context, and should also heighten children's appreciation and enjoyment of the book.

Through a regular diet of picture books — re-reading and savouring them at later stages — children can be encouraged to absorb something of the ways writers manipulate language for effect. By the time they leave primary school some children might be deepening their understanding of language through writing about picture books. Certain picture books might positively encourage them in this direction. The chapter 'Playing Around with the Familiar' suggests how writers like Anthony Browne and Fiona French might be used to help children develop their use of language through modernising and parodying traditional stories. Other picture books, like *The Jolly Postman* and *Dr*

Xargle's Book of Earthlets, can also support such development. Through the enjoyment of the rhyme, the impact of the visual, and the sheer fun of taking out and re-inserting in the envelopes all the paraphernalia that the postman delivers to well-known characters, children encounter a range of writing for different purposes and audiences. Their understanding of such uses of language increases as they get older. In particular, the brochure to the Wicked Witch, the letter and book to HRH Cinderella, and the solicitor's letter to the Wolf will seem funnier as their experience of language develops. Older primary age children might well be able to extend their understanding of the brochure and book about Cinderella through written parody but they are unlikely to appreciate fully the solicitor's letter to the Wolf. Only late in secondary school might children be capable of parodying the solicitor's language and style of writing.

Books like *Dr Xargle's Book of Earthlets* are appreciated by young children because of the funny pictures and the fun of looking at a familiar situation with fresh eyes. However, the older the children the more they get out of this book, especially if they reflect on why it is so funny (illustration 38). They might be invited to compile their own collaborative vesion of, say, a book on 'Earth Moolets'. Discussion might bring out the following points: Dr Xargle's inappropriate use of language because he misunderstands appearances, describing an Earthlet as folded in half; his misapplication of alien termino-

(38)

logy, so that he calls the arms of human babies 'tentacles'; his serious, knowledgeable teacher chalk-and-talk-manner; the contrast between his formal use of language and the pictures themselves; and (something that secondary children might appreciate) language that sounds as though it has been translated. Even after such discussion, ten and eleven year olds could still find it hard to understand that although Dr Xargle is an acute observer of events on planet earth, he lacks inside knowledge of what is really going on and is restricted by his alien terminology. That some can appreciate it, however, is clear from their writing:

> At birth an earth whalet is twenty-five tentacles long.
> (Ruth & Michelle, age 10)

> One sport earthlings play involves throwing a tiny planet at a launch pad. The earthling holding the launch pad tries to orbit the planet but the planet always returns to the green patch on which the earthlings stand. The earthlings run very fast to try to stop the planet crashing on the patch.
> (Ben, age 10 and Gareth, age 11)

> Good morning class. To-day we are going to learn about Earth Moolets.
> When they are born earth moolets are ejected from the rear-end of large moos and they come wrapped in a transparent disguise. The large moo uses a long pink tentacle to lick up the disguise so that it can be re-cycled for future use.
> (Helen, Russell, Robert, Victoria, Kevin, Jessica, Laura — age 11)

There is a precarious balance between maintaining the enjoyable experience of language the picture books provide, while also developing children's awareness of language by occasionally making explicit how it is being manipulated. It is crucial that teachers achieve that balance: pupils have so much to gain.

CHAPTER 7

A Picture Book for Life:
John Brown, Rose and The Midnight Cat

John Brown, Rose and The Midnight Cat is a gentle and apparently simple story. It epitomises what a splendid picture book can offer readers. Not only is it open to interpretation — a hallmark of a good picture book — but it also invites a response at the symbolic level.

An interesting video[1] of the book offers one possible interpretation of the story. The careful selection of aspects of the pictures, the close-ups and panning, and the order in which the pictures are shown, help support a reading of the printed text that invites sympathy for Rose, the old widow in the story. Emphasis is immediately placed on her widowhood by the first frame of her husband's car, now unused and covered up in the garage, followed by a close-up of her husband's photograph on the mantle shelf. Because of this emphasis the viewer is led to see the dog, John Brown, in a substitute role. This prepares the viewer for a very deliberate moment later in the story, when the camera pans across from the side of the double bed where Rose lies to the empty space beside her. The loneliness and frailty of her position is heightened by this treatment and provocatively exploited in a later frame. Rose's vulnerability is suggested in a close-up in which she is holding her hands up to her face, apparently shocked by John Brown's refusal to let in The Midnight Cat, and is further emphasised by the narrator's truculent tone.

Such emphasis allows for a sympathetic view of Rose's treatment of John Brown later in the book. At first she cannot induce him get up to let in The Midnight Cat but ultimately she finds a way to make him do so of his own accord rather than be forced. This reading implies that John Brown's jealousy is akin to sibling rivalry and that he needs to understand that he won't be loved any less if he shares Rose with The Midnight Cat; that however loveable, he is no substitute for a husband and that Rose needs love from as many sources as possible; that Rose has needs, represented by The Midnight Cat, beyond the immediate family circle; that John Brown's love is familiar, even boring and predictable, whereas the more self-contained and mysterious quality of The Midnight Cat attracts Rose. A feminist interpretation might be that John Brown is the typical male figure, at once domineering and pretty useless (note the mice under his chair while he is insisting that 'you don't need a cat'), and wholly dependent on Rose for his food.

An alternative interpretation is sympathetic to John Brown because of his total devotion to Rose. This is reinforced by Rose's words to him: 'We're alright, just the two of us, you and me' (illustration 40). This unsolicited remark raises questions about her subsequent behaviour towards him. Firstly, by feeding The Midnight Cat, even outside the house, Rose is disregarding John Brown's feelings and the normal antagonism between dog and cat. Actually telling John Brown to get up and let The Midnight Cat into the house is asking for trouble. Secondly, denying John Brown his food and retiring to bed pretending to be ill is no less than emotional blackmail to compel him to give in. Thirdly, Rose gets up with apparent alacrity the moment the cat comes into the house. She allows it to take over the chair John Brown always sits in and she beams at it from the other chair while apparently ignoring John Brown. This reading suggests that the book is concerned with a basic human weakness: Rose is never satisfied with what she has but must always be wanting something else. She has a loving dog, a loyal and a faithful companion, but as soon as she sees The Midnight Cat she wants it. What will she want next when the novelty wears off — a rabbit? a donkey?

The Midnight Cat itself arouses conflicting responses that in some ways complement these constrasting interpretations. In a pro-Rose reading the cat might be viewed as Rose sees it — beautiful and desirable. Certainly it has an air of mystery, conveyed by both its name and how it is described. It could be seen as representing aspects of life beyond the comfortable and secure, aspects which interest Rose and invite change (illustration 41). Or The Midnight Cat could be viewed in a more sinister light, as a threatening force from the darkness, coming to intrude and disturb. The way that it comes closer and closer to the house until it finally appears at the window silhouetted against 'the ragged sky', suggests an irresistible force, which eventually overcomes John Brown and ousts him from Rose's

(40)

(41)

husband's chair. Like Rose, the triumphantly purring cat gets what it wants — at John Brown's expense. John Brown is an Old English sheepdog — a breed that evokes traditional values of devotion, trustworthiness and faithfulness. Would the messages be the same if he were portrayed as a Yorkshire terrier, a rottweiller or a miniature poodle called Rover?

Very young children respond to the shaggy warmth of John Brown (the Dulux paint advert helps!) and reason that he cannot see The Midnight Cat, not because he is being awkward and deliberately not looking in the right direction but because his hair is in the way! Even though the thread of their feelings about him tends to be lost in their many references to dogs of their own and those of old people they know, they generally see John Brown as a cuddly and friendly dog who would be nice to stroke. Older primary school children express similar feelings, the more so because they dislike Rose's treatment of him. However, the four year old's notion of The Midnight Cat as a comfortable, nice, un-threatening black pussy differs notably from the ten year old's view of it as 'creepy': 'It looks skulky, it's got slanted eyes and it looks sly'. Yet they do not perceive the cat's movement towards the house as threatening:

> The cat hadn't got nowhere to sleep
> (Kirsty, 4 years).

Perhaps it used to live there before
(Gareth, 10 years).

Before beginning to read the story, children could be invited to consider whether or not Rose should have asked John Brown to get up and let The Midnight Cat into her house. This opens up the possibility that there might be conflicting interpretations of the book:

No, she was wrong because he didn't like
the cat
(Richard, 4 years).

Yes, I think that she's right because the cat
hadn't got nowhere to sleep
(Natalie, 4 years).

Considering this matter also allows young children to begin engaging with the story on a deeper level than usual. Normally they respond to John Brown first in relation to their own or someone else's dog. This is an important first stage in making meaning, but the question appears to move Laura (age 4) significantly beyond it when she observes:

They needed more people. She needs a dog
and a cat and to be friends with each other.
They have to be friends, if they're not
friends they'll fight with each other.
Stephen's going to play with me when we
have our lunch and then we'll go out to play
when Stephen's finished — Kirsty's going
to take the Ghostbusters down to dinner,

eat all our sandwiches up and then go out
to play.

Young children's talk is full of such apparent non-sequitors but in fact Laura seems to be making meaning for herself by linking what she understands of the text with what she has learned from personal experience. Her thinking is profound for a four-year-old and is reinforced by the attention she sustains towards the book and her own experience.

The contradictory nature of Richard and Natalie's interpretations is echoed in the responses of older children to the same question:

No, for a start the cat doesn't live there, and
John Brown does. Somebody could have
lost that cat and she'd have it in the house
and they would be wondering where it was
(Lisa, 10 years).

I would say yes because Rose was probably
too lonely and she wanted more company
(Gareth, 10 years).

Apart from Lisa's greater verbal sophistication and her ability to extend Natalie's reading of the subtext ('The cat hadn't got nowhere to sleep'/'Somebody could have lost that cat and she'd have it in the house and they would be wondering where it was'), she also illustrates an older child's growing awareness of the complexity of moral issues. This becomes more evident when the teacher challenges Gareth's response and Jamie (10 years) intervenes:

Teacher:	*Yes, but what about Rose's feelings for John Brown... you say she was lonely and wanted company, wasn't she satisfied with John Brown?*
Jamie:	*She liked John Brown but she also liked the cat. She couldn't just dump John Brown because John Brown took care of her...*
Gareth:	*'Cos like I've got — we've got two cats but I want a dog but we can't because the cats would probably run away because we've had them for a couple of years.*

At one level Jamie and Gareth together are only doing what four year old Laura did on her own: bringing their personal experience to their reflections on the text. But we can also see a level of awareness of the dilemmas entailed in moral decisions.

Four year old Ruth responded to this question and another designed to stimulate children's thinking: Should the story be read in a way that wholly favours John Brown or wholly favours Rose, or in some other way? Ruth felt that Rose had every right to ask John Brown to get up and let in The Midnight Cat, and went on to say that:

> Rose was probably trying to make John Brown share more of his heart with the cat than just her.

It is possible that Ruth was anticipating a view often expressed by adult readers, who suggest that Rose was trying to make John Brown come to a decision himself that would help him realise that Rose still loved him even when the cat was there. Ruth, like the others in her group, nevertheless disapproved of the way Rose tried to persuade John Brown to do what she wanted:

> She kind of pretended to be ill...she conned him a lot...he never had any food that day 'cos of Rose.
> (illustration 42)

Helen (11 years) observed that:

> Rose could have said something nice and reassuring to John Brown to make him feel more that he wasn't going to lose his place, he wasn't going to be kicked out because Rose wanted a cat.

Their feeling that Rose could have handled the situation more subtly and encouraged John Brown, led inescapably to Rose being perceived less sympathetically. But Helen was rather uncomfortable with this interpretation because she saw John Brown as a very stubborn dog.

Teacher:	*Why was he so stubborn I wonder?*
Helen:	*Because he wanted Rose all to himself.*
Mark:	*'Cos Rose had said earlier 'Just you and me'.*

Thea: *He thought the cat was threaten-ing him.*

Matthew, another ten year old in the group, went further, advocating a pro-Rose, anti-John Brown reading of the story:

Matthew: *I was a bit angry with John Brown because he can share the house with the cat and get along with it.*

Teacher:

So in your reading you want the audience to feel a bit annoyed with John Brown?

Matthew: *Yeh...*

Teacher: *That he's being silly? Don't let me put words in your mouth if you don't...*

Matthew: *Childish.*

Teacher: *Childish? And that he needs to ac-cept that Rose needs the cat? So how would you have to read it?*

Helen:	*Make John Brown talk in a cross, rough way.*
Teacher:	*Yes...so that's the way you'd read it...but what about Mark's point ? Rose actually said to John Brown 'We are alright, John Brown, just the two of us, you and me'. You see Matthew has possibly got a problem..he's saying that John Brown is a bit of a pain..he's moving towards the second reading. But he's got this page to overcome: 'We are alright, John Brown, just the two of us, you and me'. So how are you going to read that page so as not to make it sound very loving and kind?*

By being invited to experiment with two possible ways of reading the story and to defend their ideas, the children began to realise that the story was not straightforward. Their ambivalent feelings began to echo the tension within the book itself. Helen, showing the maturity of someone able to see more than one point of view, came to the conclusion that to do justice to the story, what was needed was somehow to 'put both readings together'.

Their ambivalence towards the characters shaped their ideas about the way the story ends. Helen and Thea viewed the story from opposite angles, yet both felt that the story did not end happily:

Helen:	*John Brown could have saved himself a lot of trouble the second time by taking notice and just letting*

	the cat in and then Rose, I don't know — they could have all lived happily together.
Thea:	*If Rose had been nicer to John Brown and tried to explain to him, then there'd have been a different ending where they all lived happily ever after.*

Children's reflections on the ending can be enhanced by asking them to note the positions of The Midnight Cat, John Brown and Rose, and the expression on Rose's face, on the penultimate page, and to consider how they would read 'and purred' on the final page (illustration 43). They can also be asked why they thought Rose wanted The Midnight Cat in the first place, and reflect on their initial feelings about the cat in the light of what happens later. They might hypothesise about what happened next and possibly write a sequel to the story. Going beyond the limits of the book can draw out the children's understanding of the story still further. One ten year old boy imagined that John Brown was cast out and living all alone in the wood behind the homestead, and saw Rose shift from hugging him early in the story, to ignoring him at the end while she gazed lovingly at the cat.

The creative response that arises naturally from a sharing of the book, might be extended by discussing the video again. Not surprisingly, most children do not notice that the opening sequence of the pictures has been altered. The narration starts with the opening lines of the story but the first frame focuses on a small detail of the large picture spread across pages ten and eleven. There are other slight modifications and emphases in the film which need to be noted. Careful questioning can encourage older primary children to think why the director began the film with that detail and how it affects the audience's feelings about Rose. Once the children recognise how the director can manipulate the response of the audience, they might want to explore how they would control the audience's response to The Midnight Cat if they were filming the book:

Jamie:	*I'd start close-up and I'd start to move....*
Teacher:	*(interrupting) Where would you have the close-up?*
Ruth:	*The eyes, the eyes.*
Jamie:	*Just around the face, facial expressions.*
Teacher:	*Why would you start on the facial expressions?*
Jamie:	*Because the cat looks sort of sleek, sort of Midnight and sly...*
Lisa:	*When they're on movies, like monsters, they start from their eyes.*

Following small, manageable experiences like these, ten year olds might move on to other picture books that are open to interpretation (e.g. Jan Mark's *Fun*). After they discuss it among themselves and share their interpretations with the teacher, they might focus on selected sections and make their own video.

43

John Brown, Rose and The Midnight Cat has clearly offered even young children a significantly rich experience and will offer more on a later revisiting. In particular, the distinctive portrayal of the three characters and their relationshop with one another encouraged the children to reflect on their own experience and to make moral judgements when they tried to understand the characters' behaviour. Empathy and moral issues came into their exploration of how the story should be read. That the same story could be read in different ways was, we suspect, an important new learning experience. While they made that discovery, the children were practising talking and reading for a purpose, and were required to use the text as evidence, wrestling with meaning in the book and the video, and not simply taking the text at face value.

Reference

1.   V246 Weston Woods

Conclusion

Although the National Curriculum endorses the importance of picture books at an early stage and recommends that favourites be revisited, many parents, teachers and children are still likely to dismiss them as too simple for older children. The National Curriculum does little to challenge this view.

We have demonstrated that good picture books sensitively presented by teachers can contribute to the development of children's thinking throughout the primary years and beyond. Indeed, the ten and eleven year olds we worked with sometimes approached a level of attainment comparable to what is required for the study of adult literature, not to picture books. The resources may be different but the skills the readers are acquiring are the same.

Children can certainly progress to adult novels but this does not mean that picture books merely represent a stage to be passed through and left behind. The potential of certain picture books for stimulating early development of sophisticated reading skills should not be lost. Reading adult novels does not necessarily guarantee that these skills will be acquired; picture books that operate on a level at which children can cope might be more conducive to learning.

David Lewis (1990) observes how picture books anticipate certain *avant-garde* adult novels by questioning the way reality is normally represented in fiction. The authors/illustrators of picture books can exploit and manipulate the interplay between text and picture.

I have argued that many of our most popular and acclaimed picture books possess highly distinctive features that are seldom fully and specifically acknowledged. I have suggested that these features might be best characterised by the way they deviate from, or cut across, the ubiquitous conventions of realist fiction.... Many metafictive picture books prise open the gap between the words and the pictures, pushing them apart and forcing the reader/viewer to work hard to forge the relationship between them. Sometimes the gap is wide enough for the relationship to remain wholly indeterminate (Lewis, 1990 p.141).

The picture books examined here address a wide range of human experience. Children experience emotions as deeply as adults do. They can become totally involved in the books and can reflect on their own experiences and empathise with the experiences and feelings of others. Picture books that are open to interpretation, that have more complex stories and no single explicit point of view are especially useful. Children will, however, have to be alerted to the interplay between picture and text and to read the subtext. Lewis stresses the need for readers to be sensitive to the ways meaning is represented in picture books. Margaret Meek (1988) also emphasises the importance of the experience that picture books can offer. She explores readers' awareness of how the books work and how children engage emotionally with the characters and situations depicted. She leaves us in no doubt that good picture books are of real value:

> Read them with your most adult awareness of life and literature and text, and you will see that the invitations they offer to young readers are far from infantile. Children who encounter such books learn many lessons that are hidden forever from those who move directly from the reading scheme to the worksheet (Meek, 1988 p.19).

References

Lewis, D. (1990) *The Constructedness of Texts: Picture Books and the Metafictive*, *Signal* Number 62 Pages 131-146, Thimble Press.

Meek, M. (1988) *How Texts Teach What Readers Learn*, Thimble Press.

Appendix 1
10-11 year olds discussing
Not Now Bernard

First section: Group on their own

1. Harry: *I don't reckon there is a monster, he's just making it up sort of thing...'cos look he passes his Mum and everything, that's why at the end he said 'I'm a monster' 'cos he's just being stupid I reckon.*

5. Kevin/Kate: *Yeh, yeh.*

6. Hannah: *No kid's like that, they like to play — they do.*

7. Kate: *A bit like Harry really.*

8. Kevin: *Harry likes to play about.*

9. Harry: *Yeh, so do you...I like it when he's got a bandage on his finger from his last accident, that's good that bit. I like the colour of his face as well, one minute it's white and the next minute it's purple (laughter, indistinguishable) and green on the end of it (laughter). That's a good one.*

14. Hannah: *They don't care by the looks of things.*

15. Harry: *No, they don't care I reckon.*

16. Hannah: *They don't look around, they're ignoring him all the time.*

17. Kevin: *He walks along smiling talking to them he goes 'hello Dad, hello Dad', 'Not now Bernard'. Bernard's probably that dog you get in the dog book.*

20. Rebecca: *His mother and his father never look round to see who it is do they?*

22. Harry: *That's the whole point (I'm going to eat you). They don't look any of the time... he doesn't know it's Bernard, it could be anybody and so I reckon — he doesn't look at him directly (they're not looking at him — his mother doesn't his Mum not looking at him there — the monster) (indistinguishable).*

27. Hannah: *Then the minute the monster eats him up and goes indoors.*

28. Harry: *And then while Dad's reading the paper he ignores...yeh, again painting (indistinguishable).*

30. Harry: *I mean that just...that's what the book's all about I reckon.*

31. Kevin: *...a monster with Bernard's head playing cricket.*

32. Kate: *You can just see a leg going away, and then up here the monster eats all of the food and watches TV.*

34. Hannah: *Yeh, how could a monster, how did a monster eat the food 'cos (in his mouth!) I know but (laughter...) he's never seen it and he's never seen his television before.*

37. Kate: *I know but that's why he's on the top of the television because he doesn't know what it is (interruptions).*

39. Hannah: *But how come he got into bed? And how come he drank the milk? (interruptions).*

41. Hannah: *Yeh, how did he know where that was?*

42. Harry: *He didn't his Mum brought it (interruptions). Well it isn't terribly realistic is it?*

44. Rebecca: *It is, it is um Bernard.*

45. Kevin: *Yeh, the teddy bear's waving his arms (interruptions...) Pretending to be a monster.*

47. Kate: *Yeh, the monster is Bernard because the monster wouldn't know like how, what you're meant to do with the TV, what you're meant to do with a comic (interruptions).*

50. Harry: *What it proves is...(interruptions) what it proves is...(more interruptions) what it proves is (yet more*

interruptions) — she might have changed her clothes or something — no but what it proves is that he might as well be a monster, his parents wouldn't know the difference...(interruptions).

54. Kate: ...'cos it might be something like a stranger in the house and they just wouldn't notice (interruptions) they just don't care... well I suppose they do care, but they're just too busy with other things (interruptions).

58. Harry: Well he's hardly been too busy with other things there and stuff is he? (Pointing to page where Bernard's Dad is reading the newspaper) (interruptions...)

60. Kate: It doesn't have to be realistic though 'cos it is for little ones and they wouldn't understand.

62. Rebecca: You know he broke the dish er right?...That meant he was angry because he was being ignored, Bernard was probably angry (because he was being ignored) yeh...and how could a monster read?

64. Kevin: Yeh...

65. Rebecca: Yeh...and how could a monster read?

66. Harry: No, he's just looking at the pictures...that's what I used to do when I was little (interruptions and giggles).

68. Hannah: Awful wallpaper, I mean look — green paint (interruptions).

69. Harry: Ah, ah that's a point — no but that might be in a ... different wall.

71. Kevin: In a bedroom they'd be more...

72. Harry / Kate: Hey! look..there — look that's his bedroom — that's one colour, that's another colour and that's another colour.

74. Kevin: And you'd notice you'd have more things in a bedroom than just a chair.

76. Rebecca: And look there's another different colour (interruptions).

77. Kevin: Yeh but you'd have more colour — you'd have more things in a bedroom as well.

79. Harry: No.

80. Kevin: You would.

81. Hannah: No, because he was ignored.

83. Hannah: How would he know where his bedroom was? How would a monster know where the bedroom was?

85. Harry: Ah, he's probably, he's got his milk in there so he follows the scent!...no, but I reckon that just proves that he's ignored.

87. Rebecca No maybe, maybe...(interrupted).

88. Kate: ...He's just kind of like, they do care but they're just too busy with other things.

90. Harry: No (interrupted) no, I don't reckon they care the they just don't bother because, because that proves he might as well be a monster (interruptions).

93. Rebecca: I reckon he dressed up in a monster suit and pretended to be a monster...trying to attract attention.

95. Harry: Like when he said there's a monster in the garden and it's going to eat me.

97. Kevin: No but they're just those sort of...tropical things...(interrupted) look it says 'There's a monster in the garden and it's going to eat me said Bernard, and then it says 'Not now, Bernard' — so that's — he's just trying to get... he (interrupted).

102. Kate: A proper, a really caring Mum and Dad would go along with it and imagine it was there.

104. Harry: Yeh, they'd make a joke of it.

105. Rebecca: Yeh, yeh (interruptions) 'Is there really?! Oh, gosh!'

106. Kate: Yeh, they'd go: 'Is there really?! I bet you'd better stay in doors' or something like that. (interruptions and giggles).

108. Harry: No, but look it says...they don't really care (interrupted).

109. Kevin: And you wouldn't have a carpet that looks like that either.

110. Harry: Look, look we're not meant to get the defects, we're meant to be arguing about it.

112. Kevin: I am arguing about it, you don't get carpets like that!

113. Kate: I reckon, I reckon that they do care but they're just too busy with other things.

115. Harry: I don't reckon it means that...

116. Kevin: Well they've got three chess boards anyway.

117. Kate: 'Cos I mean if they didn't really, if they really didn't care they wouldn't even have any toys like that would they?

119. Harry: No, I mean that isn't caring, they just say to him 'Here's some money go and get some toys' they couldn't be bothered... (interruptions to tell Hannah to shut up, to reprimand Kevin, to go back to pictures which have caught their attention and to re-read the text).

121. Harry: *No, but Kate's, Kate's right when she said that — you're right when you said that — what did you say you said um (what?) about a good parent would go along with it, I mean now at our age if I said to my Mum, that there's a monster in the garden she'd just ignore me because she'd think that I was just being stupid, but at that age 5 or 6 you'd go along with it...*

127. Hannah: *(interrupting) No, not that, I think 4 or 5...*

128. Harry: *4 or 5 you'd say 'There's a monster in the garden and he's going to eat me up' and you'd say 'Oh no! I'll go and get a gun and blow its head off'.*

Second section: teacher joins group

131. Teacher: *Do you think that you could tell me some of the conclusions that you came to?*

133. Harry: *We reckon that, or I reckon, I don't know about the others they might join me but it proves that the parents don't take any notice 'cos he might as well be a monster or anything they just don't notice.*

137. Kate: *Well, I think they care but they're just too busy to take any notice of him.*

139. Rebecca: *I think that er it is the monster's Bernard, but they've changed Bernard into a monster to make the story more exciting.*

141. Kate: *Hannah thinks he's in a costume.*

142. Teacher: *What do you think Kevin?*

143. Kevin: *A bit the same as Harry's just the same sort of thing, I reckon they just ignore him a lot.*

145. Harry: *Yeh, 'cos he might as well be anything and they wouldn't care.*

146. Teacher: *You say that they, they don't care about him but they (pointing to picture of meal on table near television)...*

147. Kate: *I think they do but they're just too busy.*

148. Harry: *I reckon because Kate said, Kate says they have toys and things but I reckon (interrupted)...just give him the money.*

150. Kevin: *It's in totally different rooms, there look.*

151. Harry: *Who cares.*

152. Kate: *Exactly, that's the kitchen and she puts it in the lounge doesn't she?*

154. Teacher: *I'm showing you those pictures because you said that Bernard's parents don't care for him.*

156. Harry: *No, I don't reckon they do because — someone's said they do care because they have toys but that isn't the point because they could just give him the money and tell him to go and buy comics or toys...they don't really care.*

160. Kate: *They do care but they're too busy at that moment — so if there's a monster in the garden they just play along with it.*

162. Harry: *Yeh, yeh they should play along with it but they can't be bothered.*

164. Kate: *...but I think they do care but they're just too busy.*

165. Teacher: *Er...you see...why did you think I was showing you those pictures?*

167. Harry: *Because he isn't looking or anything there.*

168. Rebecca: *No, they they 'cos um the mother's making the food for him.*

169. Kate: *If they didn't care they wouldn't bother about making the food for him.*

171. Harry: *No, but they have to make food for him I mean they've got to make food for him they can't just, it doesn't mean they care if they make food for them or give them toys, caring's about loving them and stuff not just giving them toys and giving them food (interrupted)...and going along with his little jokes.*

176. Kate: *But they wouldn't buy him comics and toys...*

177. Hannah: *...and he smashed that up because he was so angry that no one was taking any notice of him.*

179. Teacher: *Yeh...is Bernard, is Bernard a monster?*

180. Harry: *No...yeh a little monster.*

181. Rebecca: *He is in the story but he's himself (interrupted) but they've changed him to make it more exciting.*

183. Teacher: *Right...fine you've got some good ideas. I'm just finding it a little bit difficult because I can't, I want to listen to somebody and somebody else is jumping in, but I want to give you chances to talk.*

187. Harry: *I reckon he isn't a little monster like they call him, you know they say 'Oh my kid, he's a little monster' and things, I don't reckon he's that, it's just that he doesn't get any attention and that so he just...they think he's a little monster because they haven't got any time for him and they don't really care much about him so he would but...*

193. Teacher: *Look at that Kevin, is he a little monster?*

194.   *Kevin: No, 'cos he wasn't doing any-thing there, it's just that his Dad missed the nail... (laughter)... his Dad missed the nail and hit his finger.*

197. Harry: *No, but he didn't mean to do that did he, he didn't mean to, it's not as though he's killing him by taking off his shoes or beating him.*

200. Hannah: *Nobody was taking any notice of him so he changed into a monster.*

201. Kate: *(laughter) He's got supernatural powers so if he gets angry he can change into a monster.*

203. Harry: *(laughter) Very good Kate.*

204. Teacher: *Look at, look at the moment that he's chosen to talk to his Dad.*

205. Harry: *Yes as soon as his Dad's hitting a nail in — yeh look at his eyes, his eyes are watching (interruption) no I don't reckon now (interruption) I think I've changed, I've changed.*

208. Kate: *He didn't just think 'Oh, I'll make my Dad hit his finger with the hammer', he just, he just did it by accident.*

209. Harry: *No, I don't reckon.*

210. Teacher: *Alright, now that's the conclusion you've come to (interrupted) don't shout out but just look at the next page...look at the moment that he's chosen to ask his mother.*

213. Harry: *Looking at the cupboard (laughter... indistinguishable).*

214. Kate: *I think he just, kind of just, It's by coincidence.*

215. Hannah: *He just wants a bit of attention.*

216. Harry: *No...No.*

217. Hannah: *He just wants a bit of attention, he just wants a bit of attention, because all they're saying is 'Not now Bernard', I mean he could be coming in to help her.*

221. Teacher: *You don't think he's enjoying the mo-ment?*

222. Harry: *Yeh...I do.*

223. Hannah: *No...*

224. Teacher: *So you're changing your mind now?*

225. Harry: *Yeh, he walks off innocently sort of thing look (interrupted).*

226. Hannah: *He goes to see, he goes to say hello to his father and then he goes out, goes into the kitchen to say hello to his mother and his mother putting his (in-terrupted).*

230. Harry: *It's because... it's because he's ignored that he wants to do things like that just for a good laugh 'cos he can't do any-thing else.*

234. Teacher   *Harry's beginning to change his mind I notice...it's because he's ignored that he's wanting to do things on purpose for a laugh whereas before Harry was saying no he was innocent.*

239. Harry: *Yes, but inside he might be...because he'll get told off even more if he goes hah! hah! hah!*

242. Kevin: *Yeh (laughs).*

243. Teacher: *Because he does choose some odd mo-ments to talk to his parents doesn't he...*

245. Harry: *And when she's watering the plant and cracks the vase.*

247. Teacher: *Um...Alright shall we have it at that moment then? I'm looking forward to hearing what you had to say, and what I'd like to do is to let you hear that — not now obviously because you need some lunch, but perhaps early next week because it will be interesting for you to hear how you got on as a group, how you help each other, how good you are as a group.*

256. Harry: *We didn't do much helping.*

257. Teacher: *What makes you say that Harry?*

258. Harry: *Well...a few arguments, not serious ones just about... (interrupted) like you said (interrupted).*

260. Teacher: *Are you suggesting that an argument isn't helping?*

261. Harry: *Yeh, I reckon it does help because (in-terrupted).*

262. Teacher: *It's worth thinking about that point that Harry's made when we listen to the tape, you know, does an argument not help, or does it in fact help. What does help good group work? Let's leave it then at that then. Thank you very much.*

Appendix 2

This is a list of some of the best picture books we know, but is by no means complete since we keep discovering new ones. Although in the minority, there are now sufficient good picture books to enable teachers to enrich the reading experience of children throughout the primary school and possibly beyond.

The picture books in bold type are referred to in the text. Many of the others have similar potential and all are worthy of a place in the classroom.

Picture Book List

A Difficult Day, Eugenie Fernandez, Picture Puffin

After Dark, Louis Baum and Susan Varley, Magnet

Alex and Roy, Mary Dickinson and Charlotte Firmin, Hippo Books

A Lion in the Meadow, Margaret Mahy, Picture Puffin

All in one Piece, Jill Murphy, Walker Books

Along Came Tom, John Prater, Red Fox

A Lovely Bunch of Coconuts, Dennis Reader, Walker Books

Angel and the Soldier Boy, The, Peter Collington, Magnet Books

Angel and the Wild Animal, The, Michael Foreman, Beaver Books

Angry Arthur, Hiawyn Oram and Satoshi Kitamura, Puffin Books

Annie Bananni, Leah Komaiko and Laura Cornell, Little Mammoth

A Proper Little Lady, Netti Hilton and Cathy Wilcox, Simon and Schuster

Are we Nearly There?, Louis Baum and Paddy Bouma, Magnet Books

Asha's Mums, Rosmund Elwin, Michele Paulse and Dawn Lee, Women's Press

A Surprise for Oliver, Susan Pooley and Audrey Chappell, Picture Lion

A Walk in the Park, Anthony Browne , Macmillan Children's Books

Babylon, Jill Paton Walsh and Jennifer Northway, Beaver Books

Badger's Parting Gifts, Susan Varley, Picture Lions

Bears in the Night, Stan and Jan Berenstain, Picture Lions

Beatrice and Vanessa, John Yeoman and Quentin Blake, Macmillan Children's Books

Benjamin and Tulip, Rosemary Wells, Picture Puffin

Boxed In, Jennifer Samuels Northway, Red Fox

Burglar Bill, Janet and Allan Ahlberg, Picture Puffin

Can't you sleep, Little Bear?, Martin Waddell and Barbara Firth, Walker Books

Cat Sat on the Rat, The, Georgie Adams and Anni Axworthy, Macdonald Children's Books

Changes, Anthony Browne, Julia MacRae

Charlie's House, Reviva Schermbrucker and Niki Daly, Walker Books

Come Away from the Water, Shirley, John Burningham, Cape

Coming To Tea, Sara Garland, Picture Puffin

Cousin Blodwyn's Visit, A Vesey, Methuen Children's Books

Day of Ahmed's Secret, The, Florence Parry Hyde and Judith Heide Gilliland, Gollancz

Dinosaurs and all that Rubbish, Michael Foreman, Picture Puffin

Dogger, Shirley Hughes, Armada

Don't Forget the Bacon, Pat Hutchins, Picture Puffin

Dora the Storer, Helen East and Katinka Kew, Macdonald Children's Books

Dr Xargle's Book of Earthlets, Jeanne Willis and Tony Ross, Red Fox

Each Peach Pear Plum, Janet and Allan Ahlberg, Picture Puffin

Eat Up, Gemma, Sarah Hayes and Jan Ormerod, Walker Books

Farmer Duck, Martin Waddell and Helen Oxenbury, Walker Books

Five Minutes Peace, Jill Murphy, Walker Books

Fourteen Rats and a Rat Catcher, Tamasin Cole and James Cressey, Picture Puffin

Francie's Day in Bed, Holly Keller, Hippo Books

Frog in Love, Max Velthuijs, Red Fox

Fun, Jan Mark and Michael Foreman, Gollancz

Geraldine's Blanket, Holly Keller, Hippo Books

Gift, The, John Prater, Picture Puffin

Goodbye Max, Holly Keller, Walker Books

Goodnight Owl, Pat Hutchins, Picture Puffin

Granpa, John Burningham, Picture Puffin

Grass is Greener, The, Jez Alborough, Macmillan Children's Books

Grumpalump, The, Sarah Hayes and Barbara Firth, Walker Books

Hansel and Gretel, Anthony Browne, Walker Books

Hansel and Gretel, Susan Jeffers, Macmillan Children's Books

Happy Birthday, Sam, Pat Hutchins, Picture Puffin

I Don't Feel Well, Franz Brandenburg and Aliki, Picture Puffin

I Want My Potty, Tony Ross, Picture Lions

I'll Take You to Mrs Cole, Nigel Grey and Michael Foreman, Macmillan Children's Books

Ice Creams for Rosie, Ronda and David Armitage, Hippo Books

Jamaica's Find, Havill O'Brien, Little Mammoth

Jasper's Beanstalk, Nick Butterworth and Mick Inkpen, Hodder and Stoughton

John Brown, Rose and The Midnight Cat, Jenny Wagner and Ron Brooks, Picture Puffin

Jolly Christmas Postman, The, Janet and Allan Ahlberg, Heinemann

Jolly Postman, The, Janet and Allan Ahlberg, Heinemann

Just Awful, Alma Whitney and Lillian Hoban, Picture Lions

Kirstie Knows Best, Anthony Browne and Annelena McAfee, Magnet Books

Let the Celebrations Begin, Julie Vivas, Bodley Head

Lighthouse Keeper's Lunch, The, Ronda and David Armitage, Picture Puffin

Lily Takes a Walk, Satoshi Kitamura, Picture Corgi

Little Pickle, Peter Collington, Magnet

Lizzie's Invitation, Holly Keller, Walker Books

Long Neck and Thunderfoot, Helen Piers and Michael Foreman, Picture Puffin

Lucy Says No, Maryann MacDonald and Susie Pritchatt, Dinosaur Publications

Meanwhile Back at the Ranch, Trinka Hakes Nobel and Tony Ross, Beaver Books

Meg's Castle, Helen Nicoll and Ian Pienkowski, Picture Puffin

Milton the Early Riser, Robert Kraus, Jose Arvego and Ariane Dewey, Hippo Books

Ming Lo Moves the Mountain, Arnold Lobel, Walker Books

Mole Moves House, Elizabeth and George Buchanan, Macdonald Children's Books

Monster Bed, The, Jeanne Willis and Susan Varley, Beaver Books

Moonlight, Jan Ormerod, Picture Puffin

Moose, Michael Foreman, Picture Puffin

Morris's Disappearing Bag, Rosemary Wells, Picture Puffin

Most Beautiful Child, The, William Papas, Oxford University Press

Moving Gives Me a Stomach-Ache, Heather McKend and Heather Collins, Oxford University Press

Mr Gumpy's Outing, John Burningham, Picture Puffin

Mr Rabbit and the Lovely Present, Charlotte Zolotov and Maurice Sendak, Picture Puffin

Mum's Strike, Marieluise Ritter, Leonard Ritter and Leon Piesowocki, Magi Publications

My Brother Sean, Petronella Breinburg and Errol Lloyd, Picture Puffin

My Grandmother has Black Hair, Mary Hoffman and Joanna Burroughes, Red Fox

Naughty Nigel, Tony Ross, Picture Puffin

Never Satisfied, Fulvio Testa, North South Books

Night After Christmas, The, James Stevenson, Picture Lion

Noisy Nora, Rosemary Wells, Picture Lion

Not Now Bernard, David McKee, Beaver Books

Not-So-Wicked Stepmother, The, Lizi Boyd, Picture Puffin

On Friday Something Funny Happened, John Prater, Picture Puffin

Once there were Giants, Martin Waddell and Penny Dale, Walker Books

Oscar Got the Blame, Tony Ross, Red Fox

Paper Bag Princess, The, Robert Munsch and Michael Martchenko, Hippo Books

Park in the Dark, The, Martin Waddell and Barbara Firth, Walker Books

Patchwork Quilt, The, Valerie Flournoy and Jerry Pinkney, Picture Puffin

Peace at Last, Jill Murphy, Walker Books

Peter's Chair, Ezra Jack Keats, Red Fox

Piggy Book, Anthony Browne, Little Mammoth

Prince Cinders, Babette Cole, Picture Lion

Rosalie, Joan Hewett and Donald Carrick, Picture Puffin

Rosie's Babies, Martin Waddell and Penny Dale, Walker Books

Rosie's Walk, Pat Hutchins, Picture Puffin

Sachiko Means Happiness, Kimiko Sakai and Tomie Arai, Children's Book Press

Sad Story of Veronica Who Played the Violin, The, David McKee, Beaver Books

Sand Horse, The, Ann Turnbull and Michael Foreman, Red Fox

Sari Games, Naina Gandhi, Andre Deutsch

Six Dinner Sid, Inga Moore, Simon and Schuster

Snowman, The, Raymond Briggs, Picture Puffin

Snow White in New York, Fiona French, Oxford University Press

Snow Woman, David McKee, Beaver Books

Somewhere in Africa, Ingrid Mennen, Niki Daly and Nicolaas Maritz, Red Fox

Sunshine, Jan Ormerod, Picture Puffin

Super Dooper Jezebel, Tony Ross, Picture Lion

Surprise Party, The, Pat Hutchins, Picture Puffin

That New Dress, Malorie Blackman and Rhian Nest James, Simon and Schuster

There's a Hippopotamus on our Roof Eating Cake, Hazel Edwards and Deborah Niland, Picture Knight Books

Tiger Who Came to Tea, The, Judith Kerr, Picture Lion

Time to Get Out of the Bath, Shirley, John Burningham, Picture Lion

Timothy Goes to School, Rosemary Wells, Picture Puffin

Titch, Pat Hutchins, Picture Puffin

To-Day was a Terrible Day, Patricia Reilly Giff and Susanna Natti, Picture Puffin

Tom and Sam, Pat Hutchins, Picture Puffin

Too Big, Holly Keller, Hippo Books

Tough Princess, The, Martin Waddell and Patrick Benson, Walker Books

Towser and Sadie's Birthday, Tony Ross, Picture Lion

Two Monsters, David McKee, Beaver Books

Up and Up, Shirley Hughes, Red Fox

Very Best of Friends, The, Margaret Wild and Julie Vivas, Bodley Head

Very Worst Monster, The, Pat Hutchins, Picture Puffin

Walt and Pepper, Lisl Weil, Picture Lion

We're Going on a Bear Hunt, Michael Rosen and Helen Oxenbury, Walker Books

When I was Little, Marcia Williams, Walker books

When the Elephant Walks, Keiko Kasza, Simon and Schuster

Wheniwasalittlegirl, Rachna Gilmore and Sally Davies, Magi Publications

Where the Forest Meets The Sea, Jeannie Baker, Walker Books

Where the Wild Things Are, Maurice Sendak, Picture Puffin

Why Do Grown-Ups Have all the Fun, Marisabina Russo, Julia MacRae Books

Wilfred Gordon MacDonald Partridge, Mem Fox and Julie Vivas, Picture Puffin

William's Doll, Charlotte Zolotov, Harper Trophy

Window, Jeannie Baker, Julia MacRae Books

You'll Soon Grown Into Them Titch, Pat Hutchins, Picture Puffin

Appendix 3
Recommended further reading

Doonan, J. (1990) *Looking at Pictures in Picture books*, Thimble Press.

Graham, J. (1990) *Pictures on the Page*, NATE.

Lewis, D. (1990) The Constructedness of Texts: Picture Books and the Metafictive. *Signal* Number 62, p.131-146.

Meek, M. (1988) *How Texts Teach what Readers Learn*, Thimble Press.

Michaels, W. and Walsh, M. (1990) *Up and Away: Using Picture Books*, Oxford University Press.

Wallen, M. (Ed) (1990) *Every Picture Tells*, NATE.

Acknowledgements

Pam Baddeley, Chris Eddershaw and Trentham Books wish to thank the following publishers, authors and illustrators for permission to use their work. We have made every effort to contact publishers but if any have been overlooked we appologise and would hope to rectify this in future editions.

Penguin

Sunshine ©

A Difficult Day © 1987 Eugenie Fernandes

A Surprise for Oliver © 1989 Audrey Chappell and Sarah Pooley

Penguin Books Ltd (USA)

One Perfect Day © 1986 John Prater

Today was a Terrible Day © 1980 Patricia Reilly Giff and Susanna Natti

The Not-so-Wicked Stepmother © 1987 Lizi Boyd

Penguin Books Ltd (Australia)

John Brown, Rose and the Midnight Cat © 1977 Jenny Wagner and Ron Brooks

Random House UK Ltd

Up and Up © 1979 Shirley Hughes

The Gift © 1985 John Prater

The Perfect Day © 1986 John Prater

On Friday Something Funny Happened © 1982 John Prater

Time to get out of the Bath, Shirley © 1978 John Burningham

Octopus Publishing Group Library

Little Pickle © 1986 Peter Collington

Heinemann Ltd

Meg's Castle © 1975 Helen Nicoll and Jan Pienkowski Nord-Süd Verlag AG

Never Satisfied © 1982 Fulvio Testa

Anderson Press Ltd

I'll Take you to Mrs. Cole © 1985 Nigel Gray and Michael Foreman

Not Now Bernard © 1980 David McKee

Dr. Xargle's Book of Earthlets © 1988 Jeanne Willis and Tony Ross

Walker Books Ltd

Hansel and Gretel © 1981 Anthony Browne

Piggybook © 1986 Anthony Browne

Why do Grown-ups have all the Fun? © 1987 Marisabina Russo

Oxford Universtiy Press

Snow White in New York © 1986 Fiona French

Harper Collins Ltd

Lucy Says No © 1987 Maryann MacDonald and Susie Pritchatt